PRAYING *for the*

MEN

in YOUR LIFE

Also by Rev. Suzan Johnson Cook

PRAYING *for the* MEN *in* YOUR LIFE

Suzan Johnson Cook

editor of the best-selling *Sister to Sister*

GRAND RAPIDS, MICHIGAN 49530 USA

ZONDERVAN™

Praying for the Men in Your Life
Copyright © 2003 by Suzan Johnson Cook and Adrienne Ingrum

Requests for information should be addressed to:
Zondervan, *Grand Rapids, Michigan 49530*

Library of Congress Cataloging-in-Publication Data

Johnson Cook, Suzan D. (Suzan Denise), 1957–
    Praying for the men in your life / by Suzan Johnson Cook.—1st ed.
        p. cm.
    Includes bibliographical references and index.
    ISBN 0-310-23627-4
        1. Christian women—Prayer-books and devotions—English.
2. Christian men—Religious life. 3. Intercessory prayer—Christianity.
I. Title.
BV4844.J65 2003
248.3'2'082—dc21

                                                                2003010151
                                                                CIP

Interior design by Susan Ambs

Printed in the United States of America

03 04 05 06 07 08 09 /❖ DC/ 10 9 8 7 6 5 4 3 2 1

To all the men in my life
and in honor of my father,
the late Wilbert T. Johnson,
a praying man

Contents

———

Daughters, Sisters, Wives, Mothers, Friends

Prayer basics for the men in our lives

> A woman can change destiny on her knees.
>
> Anonymous prayer warrior

As a daughter, sister, wife, mother of two sons, and a pastor, I know how important it is to pray for men. I also know the men in my life need a special kind of prayer, prayer that I utter to God on behalf of a man without having a man's perspective.

For such prayers to be effective, I must live in harmony with my prayers in ways that do not come easily to me as a woman. I think and feel as a woman, so I must seek the Lord, search Scripture, and talk with the men themselves in order to pray "man-sized prayers."

This little book shares what I have learned on my prayer journey for the men I love.

The First Man in My Life, My Father

As a girl, I prayed for my dad, Wilbert T. Johnson. I honor him now not only because I'm the beneficiary of his hard work, but because of Wilbert T. Johnson, I have a prayer legacy—a legacy of praying for the men in my life. He was living prayer in action. Every night, no matter what time he got home, he would fall on his knees in prayer before going to bed.

Wilbert T. Johnson was a man with a vision, ahead of his time, and because of him, I'm able to thrive in so many ways, which includes my spirituality. He went to church as faithfully as he worked, never missing a Sunday unless we were not in town. It was because of his stewardship that my path to ministry was made easier.

My dad had a very hard childhood. He came to New York from Petersburg, Virginia, raised one family—his nieces and nephews—before he met and married my mother and raised us. He was definitely the patriarch of our family and quite a bit older than most dads. As I grew up, his health began failing and he had heart trouble. For most of my young life, I saw a good man who got up very early—it was always dark—and left for work at about five or six in the morning. He was proud to be one of the first Black trolley car drivers and then became part of the New York City Transit system. He never missed a day of work in the twenty-nine years he worked for Transit and was not late a single day either.

When I was about five years old, while he worked long and hard at Transit, he started a security guard and watch guard business where we lived in Northeast Bronx. That business grew steadily and then mushroomed into one of the strongest businesses in the community. It still thrives today, forty years later, as the oldest Black family-owned business in the Bronx that has been continuously running.

When I was a little girl, I prayed for his protection as he was leaving in the wee hours of the morning: "God, protect Daddy." Those simple prayers were the beginning of this book.

As I got older, I thanked God for my dad because he sacrificed to send me to private school. Set in the economically prosperous Riverdale section of the Bronx that differed dramatically from the blue-collar working class neighborhood where we lived, the school was also different culturally. The wealthy, Jewish environment that comprised so much of my world was worlds away from my dad's.

When I came home from school, I not only gave thanks for my dad's hard-earned financial support so I could attend Fieldston, but I also prayed that he would understand his teenage daughter who was living in a new sphere moving faster than anything he had ever experienced. I prayed that he would understand and help me as I made the transition to this new territory.

My prayers were miraculously answered. When I was in ninth grade, he sent me to Spain with my classmates. He didn't have a passport of his own, but he made sure I went. My dad was marvelous! I remember saying a prayer of thanksgiving for a father, who, even though he didn't understand all the pieces, was open enough to let his Bronx-born daughter become "international" and courageous enough to take risks. Wilbert T. Johnson broadened my worldview and changed my outlook on life. His decisions shaped the kind of woman I have become. And he taught me the quiet power of prayer.

When he became very ill with heart trouble, I prayed for his health. Even then I knew the toll his working two and three jobs had taken on him. He was sick most of my teenage years, in and out of the hospital. He didn't have the benefit of the medical advancements that are now available, and we didn't have the money for specialists. I believe my dad chose to spend his money educating his children, giving them the best he could, rather than on the best medical care for himself. I specifically asked God to let my father live to see me graduate from college and begin the career goals he had worked so hard for me to accomplish. Because of him, I accelerated my learning, doing two years in one.

God said no to that prayer. Daddy made it to the first semester of my senior year, when I was nineteen. During our last visit together in the hospital, I believe he knew that everything he had worked for had been planted in good soil and would bear fruit, that I was going to be successful.

My last prayers for him were that he would not suffer and that God would let him rest. God answered yes.

I was licensed and ordained into ministry at my father's home church, Union Baptist. In 1980, many men were not ready for women in ministry, but they said, "We've got to license Sujay. She's Wilbert Johnson's daughter."

Almost all my prayers throughout my life have included thanksgiving for an exceptional family, with a father who loved me and would do anything for me. Because of him, I had a privileged child-hood that was uncommon for Black girls at that time. In my childhood relationship with the most powerful person in my little life, I experienced love, wisdom, and sacrificial provision. My relationship with my father made it easy for me to relate to a heavenly Father. Because I'm a "daddy's girl" I can confidently approach my heavenly Father in prayer for men I love and who love me.

Father Prayer 1

Every one of us has two fathers. Whether we know and relate to them or not, we have a material father and a spiritual Father. It sounds simplistic, as truths often do, but knowing who our spiritual Father is and developing a close relationship with our "Daddy-God" is what human life is about. You are likely reading this book because you already know and relate to the God of the Bible as your personal "Abba Father" (Mark 14:36, Romans 8:15, and Galatians 4:6). But you may not have enjoyed the blessings of a loving, providing, protecting natural father as I did. Less than half the women in our nation grew up having a dad like mine, and I know that without that wonderful experience I might have problems relating fully to my heavenly Father. If that is your story, as the first of many prayers you will draw from this little book, pray the prayer below. Let God begin clearing residue from your relationship with your natural father, or any other "fathers" in your life. It will help immeasurably as you pray for the men in your life.

———■———

Great God, Creator of the universe, you who made me, hear this prayer and let me—through Jesus Christ—connect with you intimately as your daughter. I yield whatever is in me that hinders our relationship, including anything involving my natural father. I leave all such hindrances at the foot of the cross, because they are sins Jesus has already handled. I trust your Spirit's work, with time, to heal me of all the results of these sins and to enlarge my capacity to be your beloved daughter and experience you as my Daddy-God.

Father Prayer 2

If, like me, you've had a great relationship with your natural father, stepfather, or surrogate dad, celebrate with this prayer:

Lord, thank you for a deeper understanding of just how important Dad has been in my life. He has given me a glimpse of you, making it easier for me to relate to you. Bless him richly! Let Dad's and my relationship be a basis for my understanding of the men on whose behalf I will offer prayer.

The Man Who Sticks Closer, My Brother

From childhood to this day I have prayed for my brother, Charles Ronald Johnson. He's six years older than I am. Even before our dad passed, we'd often take trips to North Carolina, just the two of us, starting when my brother was sixteen years old. We shared a lot during those ten- to twelve-hour car trips.

Because of my father's untimely death when I was nineteen, my brother assumed the role of a surrogate father to me. When I was in junior high, I prayed that he would be able to handle my father's illness, to step into his shoes. With the family responsibilities, he had a lot on his shoulders during his college and law school years, and he handled them admirably.

My brother has been with me in building both of the ministries God has called me to lead, so he has been a trailblazer with me. Because he's protective of me, I delicately balance my pastoral role with my sister role. When he was in his thirties, and I was a still a relatively new pastor, he became very sick and had to have major surgery.

"Sujay, come and serve me communion here in the hospital," he said by phone from his sick bed.

I remember thinking, *Oh, I really just want to be your sister.*

He wanted me to be a pastor. I did serve him communion. I also prayed for him as his pastor *and* as his sister. But then I also doted on him, little sister to big brother!

I pray varied and specific requests for my brother because we are so close, but my prayers almost always include his protection. Today, praying for protection for young men, especially Black men, is paramount. On those youthful trips down south, the police would stop my brother for no reason. (The reason now does have a name, and thankfully Congress and our law enforcement agencies have recently begun to address this problem of racial profiling.) I'd sit silently while my brother was subject to this harassment and pray that God would keep him safe from police brutality. As we continued our journey, I'd pray that God would help my brother get through the pain of insult and the anger it provoked in him.

I also pray for my brother's family. He has a wonderful wife and two children—my only niece and nephew. My prayers for him extend to them, which led me to a simple but important discovery about prayer—praying for the men in my life automatically leads to prayer that touches others.

I pray for Charles as a businessman, for his professional development, and for the success and growth of the family business. (He now runs the security business.)

I continue to pray for his spiritual growth and that he will use his talents and live God's destiny for his life. He has sought an electoral office, and I worked closely with his campaign. When he was elected, I prayed for him to be out of the way of hurt and harm and steer clear of all the evil prevalent in the political world.

Most of all, I pray that we stay a close family. We all love each other very much and our prayers are usually prayers of thanksgiving to God for providing us so much materially and spiritually.

Brother Prayer

Praying for a brother or other relative creates a bond that magnifies the blood relationship. The kinship becomes even more precious and even subtly more intimate as we pray.

If these relationships are strong and happy, thank God for them, perhaps expressing your gratitude for a shared heritage with such good men. But if, like so many families, yours includes challenging interactions with brothers, male cousins, uncles, and male in-laws, begin approaching God with a prayer like this:

———■———

Lord, you created kinship order—and have placed me in this family—for a purpose. I open myself to your intent in giving me these blood ties. As you grow me as a Christian "sister," help me to be an exemplary natural sister and remove any barriers between me and my brothers that hinder prayer and block blessings.

THE Man in My Life, My Husband

My prayers for my husband, Ronald Cook, have probably been the most intense prayers of all. I prayed for him before I knew him. I had asked God to direct me to the man I was to marry, if that were God's will for my life. Upon meeting Ron, I prayed that the Lord would steer him and confirm that we were God's match. I prayed to be sure that he was the man God sent me, and when I was sure, I thanked God for him. Now we're in our eleventh year of marriage, having grown in so many ways, and I still pray constantly.

As I watch him father our sons, I pray that he will continue to have a strong relationship with them. They play together. They wrestle together. They watch cartoons together. God daily answers my prayers for Ron as a father, and it gives me great joy!

I pray for Ron and me together. It is as if we are truly one flesh. My constant prayer is that we don't grow apart. I pray that we continue to grow together, that we will always be able to communicate both our struggles and our joys, that we will grow even deeper in our love, and that while we parent well together, we will also have time for each other as husband and wife. We are prayer partners and so I pray *with* him. I encourage wives to pray with your spouses. Pray with your boyfriend, your fiancé. It makes a difference. If you start the day in prayer and certainly if you end the day in prayer, you can't go to sleep angry. The Holy Spirit leads you to deal with your issues in prayer and then in relationship with one another.

And finally I pray that Ron will find his true purpose. He has a passion for writing, so I pray that he is able to write his book deal one day, as that's his desire.

Praying for Ron has deepened my love for him and has helped me to hear God's voice more clearly about God's will for me as a woman and wife.

Husband Prayer

Many inspired guides have been published to help wives pray for their husbands. I trust this book will provide further guidance if you are praying for your spouse, your intended, or even your "ex." The following, is a simple start, improvised from Proverbs 31:11–23 (MSG):

Lord, may my husband trust me without reserve and never have reason to regret it. May he be greatly respected.

None Compare to Prayers for My Sons

I pray for my sons, Samuel and Christopher, as intensely as I pray for Ron. Christopher is seven; Samuel is nine. As much as possible, I pray *with* them each day, but certainly every day I pray *for* them.

Like most mothers, protection is my number one concern. I worked in the White House when Al Gore was Vice President, and as he hosted a father's family conference, Tipper Gore moderated a panel of women on which I served.

"What do you pray most for your children?" Tipper asked me.

"That they live to be adults," I responded. "Having two Black boys growing up amidst the racism that's prevalent in America means I *have* to pray that they live and become strong Black men."

I ask God to protect them from hurt, harm, and danger while they're in school and for traveling mercies as they go to and from school, sports, and their other activities. I believe children should have joyous memories, and so my daily prayer is that I deliver happy children to school and pick up happy children from school. I pray that they'll know when to exhibit strength, use wisdom, and avoid situations that will bring them in harm's way. I pray that they're prepared to do whatever God's will is for their lives. I don't pray for them to be great athletes.

When Samuel was nine months old, I received a fellowship to the White House to work with the President of the United States on the Domestic Policy Council. Ron stayed in New York, while the baby and I lived in Washington. Ron and I had a commuter marriage that year, and I remember vividly that when we first arrived at our small apartment in Washington, I placed a picture in the window of Ron and I holding Samuel on his Blessing Day.

Samuel went right to the picture and cried out, "Daddy!" If you could only have seen this child—less than a year old—reach out for his dad's picture and cry!

I cried too. I sorely missed Ron, and I also realized how important family—a father *and* a mother—is to children. I realized how important men are in the lives of children.

I continually pray that we will always be a family, there to support, nurture, and strengthen our sons no matter what differences or disagreements their dad and I have. My prayer is that we will be the parents, the family, that they need us to be.

Although many women say, "I can make it without him," and many simply must, I understood from my son's baby cries the need for a father-mother family and I pray that he has it.

Another memory from those White House days is when I was traveling in a little prop plane to West Virginia. During the scary ride, I realized I could die. I thought about my child down on the ground in the White House daycare center. I prayed, asking God to keep me and allow me to be there until he became an adult. After that plane ride, I made a will and got Ron's and my affairs in order, but I pray that I can be there for and with Samuel and his brother, Chris, until they are able to stand on their own feet and that I am able to instill in them godly values.

Son Prayer

Much will follow in this book that will help mothers pray for sons, but begin with this short dedication of your son to God, inspired by Luke 1:38 (MSG):

———————

Lord God, my son was your son first. You knit him together in my womb. As much as I love him, your love for him is even greater. So, I place him before you in spirit as wholly yours. Let my attitude toward my son be as Mary's when you made her the mother of Jesus, "I'm the Lord's maid, ready to serve."

Spiritual Brothers, Colleagues in Faith

I have the privilege to pastor a church, and in that role, I pray for all the men in my church. I have so many wonderful men who surround me and my family. I pray that they will continue to grow spiritually, that they will be active in the church and not just there on Sunday mornings, and that these men will feel ownership of the ministry.

My prayer is also that I will never insult or hurt them, intentionally or unintentionally, and that I will be a pastor who is sensitive to male feelings. I also ask God to help me, if I do offend a brother, to help him forgive and not be bitter.

Two men serve on our ministry team, including my first homegrown "son" in the ministry, and I pray that the relationship between these men will grow and that the number of men in our church will grow. I pray they will find their God-given purpose and tasks and will feel free to praise God without any inhibitions and give glory to God in their lives. On any given Sunday, a third of our population of worshipers is male, in a family-oriented ministry. For me as a female pastor, it's an encouraging, wonderful atmosphere.

I'm praying for the two men on our leadership team to develop the ministries that speak to men's needs so they will grow in all of the goodness of the Lord. I pray these two men will first grow strong internally and then be able to reach out into the community to disciple other men, so they may be introduced to the Lord.

I have been blessed with many wonderful male colleagues in Christian leadership. I pray that they see us female pastors as sister-colleagues and not just women in the flesh. My prayer is that we have healthy relationships. I have several wonderful male colleagues whose entire families know my family, which is an answer to prayer that our friendships grow, not as flesh attractions, but as spiritual relationships. As we women grow in ministry, it is important to have the respect of men in ministry, and I pray constantly for that.

Recently, I had a symposium of over a hundred women in ministry. I shared with them how important relationships with men are, that we need brothers in Christ whose spirits connect with ours. There are many such men, and my prayer is that God show me how to celebrate those who are in my life. I have been so blessed to have pastor colleagues across the country who gave my ministry a start. I pray for them regularly. My own pastor, Ollie B. Welles, opened the door for my ministry.

When you understand how to show appreciation to God by honoring the godly men you know, God will send more of them into your life. God sees that you were faithful over the few and then increases and multiplies.

I've come to understand as a pastor, wife, and mother that the protection I prayed for my father and then my brother when I was a little girl was the beginning of a lifetime of prayer for the men in my life. These uniquely woman's prayers, which we share regardless of race as our men go out into a "man's world," are a gift God gives our men through us.

Every prayer is different. The same words can be uttered to God on behalf of a son and a brother and a husband, yet those words reach our Lord with different nuances of meaning, because our relationships with sons, brothers, and husbands each have their own character. Begin using the prayer formats in this book with the men closest to you and watch how your prayers conform to each relationship.

Spiritual Brother Prayer

No prayer for our brothers in the Lord compares, in my opinion, with this one, improvised from Paul's prayer for the Ephesian brethren (3:16–19):

———■———

I pray that out of your glorious riches you will strengthen my brothers in Christ with power through your Spirit in their inner beings. Christ, dwell in their hearts through faith. And I pray that my brothers, being rooted and established in love, may have power united with all of us Christians. Allow them to grasp how wide and long and high and deep is your love, Christ Jesus. Let them experience this love that surpasses knowledge and be filled with you, dear God.

One purpose for this book is to help us do the inner work in ourselves, as women, so we are in right relationships with the men in our lives. It is only then that our prayers can be powerful and effective (James 5:16).

May this book enrich your prayers so every man for whom you pray becomes a spiritual giant.

Learn

The prayer of a righteous (wo)man is powerful and effective.

James 5:16

Unlearn

I can only pray from an attitude of love and forgiveness. If I have issues with a man in my life, I can't pray for him.

Prayer 1

Lord, show me the men you want me to pray for. Enable me to pray for them. Equip me to pray for them effectively.

2

Five Reasons We Must Pray for the Men in Our Lives

Valuable results of a God-connection through prayer

Have we trials or temptations?
  Is there trouble anywhere?
We should never be discouraged;
  take it to the Lord in prayer.
Can we find a friend so faithful
  who will all our sorrows share?
Jesus knows our every weakness;
  take it to the Lord in prayer.
> "What a Friend We Have in Jesus"
> by Charles C. Converse

During a twenty-five year friendship, Eva discovered the value of prayer for herself *and* for Carter, a lifelong friend.

Eva and Carter were close friends in their bohemian artist days. Their common interest in art created an enduring, platonic bond between them even after Eva became a Christian. In her early zeal for the Lord and the church, Eva over-enthusiastically shared her new spiritual discoveries with Carter, who had no interest in religion. He reacted first with curiosity, then watched Eva stumble often and painfully. Eva eventually learned that she had no power to influence Carter, that all she could do was pray for him, a discipline she was only learning.

Eva's faith grew stronger over the years, and while Carter no longer believed evangelical Christianity to be a fad for Eva, it was not for him. Carter's life centered on artistic and intellectual pursuits, and Eva's became more traditional, full of church activities and Bible studies.

By the time they were both late in middle age, Eva's worldview had become wholly Christian, and Carter occasionally responded with anger to things she said about her religion. Still they spent time together visiting museums and galleries and discussing visual art. She tried to avoid topics that might lead to discomfort, but she found it hard *not* to share her faith. Their common ground for discussion felt smaller and smaller to Eva.

Then during a phone conversation, Carter angrily cut her off, refusing to let her express her views. Their friendship ended abruptly, without argument, as they hung up, not having made the plans they intended for a gallery visit. Eva was insulted, hurt, and angry, but relieved to be free of a friendship where she couldn't be herself—a sold-out Christian. She began to regularly pray for Carter's salvation, something she had done only sporadically over the years.

Fresh from a seminar where she had resolved to get serious about prayer, Eva made a "salvation list" of "hard cases" in a spiral notebook and established a loose routine of praying for her friends and colleagues who seemed beyond the reach of the gospel. She could not imagine how Carter, an ivy-league-educated artist who had successfully created a niche for himself in the art world, could ever view Jesus Christ as anything but a mythical icon. But her lists gave a sense of purpose to her prayers.

For more than a year they made no contact, and her relationship with Carter took on a new dimension as she "related to him" via her prayer list.

As she prayed mundanely for her hard-cases list, her hurt feelings healed and her self-righteous attitude softened. To her surprise, she began to approach the list with almost a feeling of grief. When she began, she had prayed for the snooty intellectuals from her loft of salvation. Over time, she began to remember forgotten snatches of her life and tried to imagine who she would have been if not for the few twists and turns that led her to the foot of the Cross.

Then Carter called her late one evening. She could tell he was in such pain, that he was audibly swallowing his pride. "Eva, Ma's dying. I don't think she'll make it through the night."

Eva headed right over there and when she saw him, he was not Carter, the self-assured artist. He was a man for whom the mystery of death had not been decoded by the hope of resurrection. He was a child who had not learned how to invite the Holy Spirit to provide him comfort.

Eva sat all night as his mother lay dying. She sang hymns and recited psalms to her, careful to keep her voice low and not to offend Carter, who sat listlessly in another room.

The funeral was the first time Carter had been in a church since his father had died a dozen years before, and afterward he told Eva how touched he was by the simple kindness of the congregation and pastor in burying his mother. Eva had sung the words and swayed to the rhythms of the hymns at the funeral while Carter and his artist friends stood stolid, looking like welcomed visitors to a country whose language they had neglected to learn. The pots of food had created a wonderful aroma in the basement of the old church, and Carter was visibly succored by the fellowship of his mother's church family. He said he was grateful Eva had come to the funeral. She was glad. She had felt like a native translator, helping connect him to the foreign ways and words that he so needed to grasp for comfort.

Eva had met the pastor once, years before, and gently reminded Carter that he conducted the funeral for one of Carter's friends who had died of AIDS. As they left, the pastor grasped Carter's hands and then embraced him. "This was your mother's church. Make it yours. Come back."

The pastor made Eva proud of her faith. But she could not imagine that this decrepit, working-class chapel with its unfinished basement for fellowship and Sunday school was a place Carter would return to, now that his parents were gone. She was almost as sure that she and Carter would return to divergent paths.

A few Sundays later, she returned from church to a ringing phone and was surprised to discover Carter calling. "I just came home from church and thought I'd see if you wanted to get together ..." His voice was new, 2 Corinthians 5:17 new.

"Sure," she said, restraining her urge to question him. She hung up the phone and gave a shout to the Lord.

In the weeks and months after Carter's mother died, Eva continued to pray and marvel as he talked about his church attendance. Then he found his mother's Bible and began reading her favorite Scriptures that she had marked. Eva listened and celebrated his discoveries with him. God was answering her prayer. The supernatural was taking place before her eyes. She was not to disciple, preach, teach, or compel, but to simply pray. She thought back to her first days being reborn and remembered that heady new feeling, and savored it afresh with Carter. She kept him on her hard-cases list, not wanting to ask him any questions. It was not her assignment to track his progress on his spiritual journey, only to pray for him.

Then one evening four or five months after his mother died, Carter called to tell Eva he had finally been able to check his mother's safe deposit box at the bank. "Guess what I found?"

"I can't begin to guess what you found in the box, Carter," she replied.

"My baptismal record."

"Huh?"

"My baptismal record. From 1950. I was two months old. You know what it reads? 'Carter Brown is a child of God, member of the body of Christ, and an inheritor of the kingdom of heaven.'"

Eva was stunned silent. Her soul was bearing witness to God's plan, laid half a century before, literally while Carter was being knit in the womb of his godly mother.

"Did you hear that? 'Carter Brown—a child of God, member of the body of Christ, and an inheritor of the kingdom of heaven.'"

"Yes, Carter, I heard," she said, regaining her sangfroid. "I'm talking to a child of God, member of the body of Christ, and an inheritor of the kingdom of heaven?"

"You sure are," he said.

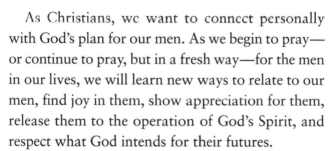

As Christians, we want to connect personally with God's plan for our men. As we begin to pray—or continue to pray, but in a fresh way—for the men in our lives, we will learn new ways to relate to our men, find joy in them, show appreciation for them, release them to the operation of God's Spirit, and respect what God intends for their futures.

This God-connection through prayer yields five valuable results:

1. *Prayer releases the power in us* (James 5:16). Prayer allows us to be stronger with and for our men.

God's Spirit draws men. We do not. Eva could not draw Carter to God. But prayer strengthened Eva to be *effective,* to be who she needed to be in Carter's life—a caring friend. Chapter 3 will expound on this personal power release.

2. *Prayer unleashes God's power and purpose in our relationships* (see 2 Thessalonians 1:11). Prayer allows all those in our lives to be affected by our faith.

God already has plans for the men for whom we are praying. Through prayer we connect ourselves to those plans, we realign our relationships according to God's script, and we receive the power we need to act our part well. Eva was trying to play a role in Carter's life that God had assigned elsewhere five decades before. Prayer gave her the power to respond when called, and the insight to stand by and let God work through others God had placed in Carter's life. Chapters 4 and 5 show how to develop the kinds of prayers that hook us into the Lord's exciting, but often late-seen, work with our men.

3. *Prayer heals wounds* (2 Chronicles 7:14). Our men are wounded by the world, by circumstances, and, yes, by us, the women in their lives. Prayer begins the healing process that allows them, and us, to go forward, forgetting what's behind (Philippians 3:13).

Eva's prayers expunged her hurt and her guilt in the soured friendship. If not for prayer, bitterness might have taken root in Eva and prevented her from responding with the love of Christ when Carter called her to his mother's deathbed. Prayer also allowed her to face her own religious arrogance and put it in check before Carter was further turned off to the Christian faith by her attitude. Praying for Carter healed Eva. God's healing via prayer is rarely like a comfortable sling, but more often a cutting incision into one of our long-harbored attitudes or emotional or mental assumptions. Chapters 6 and 7, although focused on finding the time to pray and handling God's no answers to our prayers, also touch on the healing aspect of prayer.

4. *Prayer builds a strong community and encourages others.* Praying about common concerns allows us to collectively be strengthened. In Matthew 18:20, Jesus promises us that where two or three are gathered together in his name, he will be in the midst of them. Prayer allows us to be a community with Christ's power at the center. The challenges that our men face need collective prayer that brings Christ's power into play in their lives.

At Bronx Christian Fellowship, we have invited people who live in the same geographical area or who are professionals working in the same field to create circles of prayer at church and during the week in their workplaces. These prayer partnerships have built solid Christian fellowships among law enforcement officers, educators, students, homemakers, as well as literal neighbors.

Eva discovered that she was part of a faith community God had placed around Carter, and that strengthened and made her proud of her faith. Prayer always builds community. Chapters 3, 5, and 7 reveal the community-building power of prayer—whether you believe you are praying singly about a man in your life or if you are already involved in group prayer for him.

5. *Prayer works.* When *you* have a prayer life, it brings you the "peace which transcends all understanding," regardless what the men in your life are bringing you (Philippians 4:7).

If we are praying in God's will, our prayers will be answered because God's will is indeed going to be done. But like Eva, we may need to adjust our understanding of God's will and untangle strands of our own will—our own how, how long, when, where, and why—from God's marvelous plan. Chapters 8 and 9 help us tune into God's plan and prayerfully sing along.

Making the Connection

1 Thessalonians 5:15–20 offers a simple guide to develop a prayer life that connects us with God in order to pray effectively for man-specific concerns: "Make sure that nobody pays back wrong for wrong, but always try to be kind to each other and to everyone else. Be joyful always; pray continually;

give thanks in all circumstances, for this is God's will for you in Christ Jesus. Do not put out the Spirit's fire; do not treat prophecies with contempt."

Prayer is not isolated from other aspects of our lives. It is totally in harmony with what we say, do, and are. It is part of the fabric of our lives, like a beautiful thread woven with other lovely strands to make a whole cloth.

From this Scripture in Thessalonians, we discover that our God-connection needs to include:

    Pardon

    Right relationship

  Th**A**nks

  Jo**Y**

Op**E**nness to the operation of God's Spirit

    Respect for prophecy

Pray for the men in your life, with the 1 Thessalonians 5:15–20 prayer acrostic in mind.

Prayer is an essential discipline of the Christian faith, but be careful not to confuse discipline with routine. Each of us must discover for ourselves the right amount of prayer time and the best place for prayer in our 24/7s. There is no formula for taking time with God except that there needs to be some communication every day. That does not mean the same amount of time or same time each day. Place more emphasis on the rudiments than on the routine.

Crisis Prayer

Most women pray for the men in their lives in times of challenge, fear, or disappointment—after they have tried everything else, when they realize they have no power in a situation. In the midst of a crisis, even those who don't regularly talk with God cry out for help.

As Christians, we also pray when we don't know what else to do. "The name of the Lord is a strong tower; the righteous run to it and are safe" (Proverbs 18:10). God delights when, at our wits end, we pray for our husbands, sons, brothers, and friends. But as believers, our crisis prayers are different. Our prayers are initiatives that usher in the work God wants to do in the world, and specifically in our tiny spheres of influence. The reason for our prayers is to deeply and fully connect the men we care about with God's purposes for their lives in trying times. We pray *through* situations, not just in crises.

Living a prayerful life, we take the high ground, find something to be happy about, and thank God even when we don't understand why things are occurring. Christian women know God is perfecting our men (and *us!*). We allow the Holy Spirit to operate in our lives. Through prayer, we *invite* the Holy Spirit into our relationships with men.

If you have turned to this book for some help with crisis prayers, be comforted knowing that God hears and is calling you, starting with this dire circumstance, to a lifetime of prayer.

Learn
Pray continually! Here and now is the time and place to make a God-connection for the men in your life.

Unlearn
"I have to work praying for _____ into my busy schedule."

Prayer 2
Pardon me and _____ for our sins and shortcomings.

Restore us to Right relationship with you and with each other.

ThAnks for _____
_____.

My joY overflows because of ____
_____.

Lord, I opEn myself to the work of your Spirit.

With deep Respect for prophecy, I know you will reveal to me what I need to know to pray in your will and work in harmony with my prayers.

3

Prayer Releases the Power of Change in *Us*

God answers our prayers for our men by changing us first

> To pray is to change. Prayer is the central avenue God uses to transform us.
>
> Richard Foster, *Celebration of Discipline*

Deena's prayer circle has watched with awe as God has answered her prayers for Albert by changing her.

Deena, a divorced Christian woman in her late thirties, had not had a date in eleven years when she began to pray for God's guidance regarding Albert, a mid-forties divorced father of grown children, who worked in security and attended her church. He had approached her and said, "God told me you are my wife."

The three other members of her prayer circle, which has now been meeting weekly for over six years, felt Albert an unlikely match for Deena, who worked at a major magazine and was studying Italian and poetry to earn her master's degree. They became even more dubious when Albert was fired after more than twenty years of service, with a notation that prevented him from ever working in security again. But their circle was committed to praying, so they simply prayed for God's will for Deena and Albert.

When Deena quietly married Albert, less than a year after she had first mentioned him in her prayers, the circle was happy for her because they knew her deepest desire was for a husband and family. The marriage began with Deena's husband, a smoker, moving in with her, a nonsmoker, as he undertook a court battle to receive a pension from his former employer.

Deena and her spiritual sisters prayed fervently about Albert's job situation and that he would have the strength to quit smoking. Meanwhile, Deena's gynecologist confirmed what Deena had already been told: She was unable to have children. Deena might be able to conceive if she underwent surgery, but even with the best results, her likelihood of bearing a child would be very slim.

During the first months of their marriage, Albert and Deena visited a minister who prayed with them about Albert's nicotine habit and Deena's infertility. Immediately, Albert quit smoking cold turkey. Soon after, the prayer circle's rejoicing was twofold—Deena, who was nearly forty, was pregnant. She had not had surgery or any kind of medical intervention.

Albert remained unemployed. The circle prayed with renewed faith for each prospect and interview. If God had the power to take away his desire for nicotine after an entire adulthood of smoking and to open Deena's womb, certainly God could get Albert a job before the baby was born, so she could be the stay-at-home mom she wanted to be.

Deena and her circle's prayers became intense as the delivery date approached and after the baby was born. Those fervent prayers reached a crescendo while Deena breastfed her endearing newborn during their prayer circle gatherings, as Deena's weeks of maternity leave and vacation ticked away. Their prayers were desperate while she remained home with baby Samuel on unpaid leave. Then they prayed soberly through Deena's time of decision, when her boss called to tell her that she needed to return to work or lose her job. During that time, her long-awaited joys of motherhood were tinged with disappointment that her baby's father was not the provider she had hoped and prayed for.

Deena returned to work. She was fortunate that she was able to leave baby Samuel with a licensed sitter right in her building who took care of a handful of infants and toddlers. But it broke her heart to leave Samuel with a "stranger." And every time one child had a cold, Sam came home with a cold. The costs blew her budget too. When Albert had moved in with her, her expenses had not risen by much at all, but now childcare costs made it impossible for them to live on one salary. Albert continued to have an occasional interview, but the disappointment that had been apparent in Deena's prayers for Albert subtly began to be reflected in a sour tone when she spoke to him. Then she stopped mentioning him in her prayers. The circle simply asked God to bless Albert, Deena, and Samuel and for God's Spirit to be in the midst of their new family.

Shortly after Samuel began going to the sitter, he caught a cold and needed to stay home. Albert, who had grown children and small grandchildren, was adept at caring for him. Deena, torn between relief and jealousy, soon decided that Samuel was far better off staying in their own apartment with Albert as his caretaker. With this decision, they could again comfortably manage on one salary—hers.

As Albert embraced his role as a stay-at-home dad, dramatic changes occurred in their apartment. Deena had lived in the apartment for more than a dozen years amidst piles of books and an eclectic mix of old furniture. Soon Albert built shelves; replaced the kitchen floor; painted the walls; installed ceiling fans; created a huge storage space with drawers, doors, and shelves along an entire wall; stripped molding; and repaired and restored old furniture. Over time, Albert transformed the apartment from the habitat of a busy divorcee to a charming family environment, neat as a military installment, despite toddler Samuel's myriad toys and paraphernalia.

Samuel had been on the fast track to becoming the spoiled brat of a doting, permissive, all-loving mother, and was now balanced by the discipline of a limit-setting, at-home daddy. And after a long court battle, Albert was awarded a small monthly pension.

Deena no longer prays for a job for Albert, at least not in the prayer circle. The sour tone has given way to an easy, loving banter between them as she goes off to work she enjoys and leaves the child she loves at home with the man she loves.

"Sometimes it just amazes me that I had another whole life here before Albert and Samuel," she said one day, beaming, as the circle gathered in prayer. "God has just transformed my life."

Deena commented to the circle one day as they scurried off after their hour of prayer, "Sam's growing up so fast! He's almost ready to go to preschool. And, Albert's ready to go back to work," she mentioned wistfully, with a tinge of regret at the prospect of change from what had turned out to be a very sweet phase in her life.

Deena's prayer partners watched God answer Deena's prayers for Albert in ways that are instructive for all women. God didn't answer yes to the prayers to provide Albert another job, and yet Deena is grateful to God for answering *all* of her prayers—by changing Deena.

As women, we want to change men. Admit it. God already knows our hearts.

Fill in the following blanks:

I'd like my husband to be more _____. I wish my son were more _____, my brother less _____. If only dad were _____. And it would be great if my male friend didn't _____.

You probably picked up this book because of some work you believe God needs to do in a man's life. You want to pray more effectively for him so God will work in him. If you have already been praying for him—husband, father, brother, son, close relative, friend, boyfriend, fiancé—and know praying is the right thing to do, but are not seeing a change, pray this:

Prayer 3
Lord, I know you will bring about the change I have prayed for because I am willing to be changed in whatever way you wish.

That prayer is the beginning of the work God is going to do as you pray for the men in your life.

You will pray for them, but the power of change is going to be released first in *you*. You will see the changes you desire, but you will see changes in yourself first.

When an object is lit from behind, a shadow is cast in front of it. You see the shadow of the object before you see the object itself. We're often startled when we see a shadow. That's because we see the shadow before we see who or what is casting the shadow.

Think of the results of prayer that way. The changes in us are the shadow. The man is the object. God is, of course, the light. We will likely notice changes in ourselves, in our perceptions, and in our attitudes before we see changes in the man we are praying for.

A friend of mine just had her house rewired. She returned from a weekend away to discover what she thought was a total electrical outage. Entering the large townhouse alone, she felt her way up a few steps, looking above the winding staircase into complete darkness. She wondered if there was power upstairs. As her eyes adjusted to the dark, welcomed shadows of the railings appeared on the wall. From those shadows, she knew there was light on the upper floors.

The changes in us, the shadows, let us know that God, the light, is at work even when we can't yet see the desired changes in our men. And sometimes, as in Deena's case, God's plan may be to wholly change *us* so we can see the man we are praying for the way God sees him.

God Is Already At Work

By praying for or even feeling the urge to pray for someone, we can rest assured that God is already at work. God has already begun working in the situation, starting with us. In even our basic prayers for protection or for salvation, God is working to change us.

There are two ways that we know immediately that God is working in the lives of those we pray for. First, our own feelings are transformed when we pray. Eva's self-righteousness became compassion. Deena's judgment of Albert was transformed to appreciation. And second, we are infused with power when we pray. Eva received the power to be still, the self-control and humility to let God work. Deena was empowered to accept the traditional role reversal.

A range of emotions from anxiety to hopelessness might have brought us to our knees to pray, but the act of prayer changes those feelings. We arise empowered to rest in God, confident in a God-specified outcome.

Read this prayer (based on 2 Timothy 1:7) out loud:

Prayer 4
Lord, you have not given me feelings of fear
or of [add your own feelings], but you have given
me a sense of power, love, and mental stability.

Before we explore the men in your life and the
issues you want to present to God on their behalf,
before we explore the various kinds of prayer for
men, before we find the words to articulate our
thoughts and feelings to God, before we learn how
to recognize God's voice in answer to our prayers,
we must accept that God is going to answer our
prayers by changing us.

We will have a power released in us that we know
is more than our own strength. We will have attitudes and mental states that were impossible for us
to maintain in previous circumstances. We will stand
and face issues that once backed us away. If we fervently pray, these are the first results we will see.
These will be the shadows of things to come, things
God will do in the man for whom we are praying.

And like shadows, these things may disappoint
us. We may feel let down when God works in us
and we don't yet see God working in the man. Have
you ever been waiting for someone driving a cer-
tain make of car and seen a shadow approaching
that heightened your anticipation, thinking it was
the one coming to pick you up? As it sped by rather
than slowed down, your heart sank. As God works

in us, we might think, *Thanks, God. I needed that. I needed peace of mind and that loving attitude. But would you please get on with making* him *do the right thing?*

God is not going to change the men in our lives. No matter how much we pray and even fast and meditate on Scripture, God still is not going to change *them* because we pray. Our prayers for them will change *us,* and through us miracles will be set in motion. Prayer allows us to be stronger with and for our men.

When God Says No

When God says no, it is easy to give up and stop praying. Think about Deena going back to work when she had prayed so hard for Albert to get a job so she could stay home.

Before we give up, we must remember that hearing from God is awesome in itself. We're relating to the sovereign Creator and Maintainer of the universe! We're in communication; now is no time to shut down. Rather, it is time to learn how to receive the results God intends.

God's intentions for the men we are praying for are infinitely greater than our intentions for them. If God has said no, it is time to relate to God even more to find out what God's greater intentions are.

When God answers no, our challenge is to discover the question for God's yes.

God answers prayer, and when we learn to pray, God will release power in our lives, whether it's for a job, marriage, finances, anything and everything. But we must be willing to accept the answer God gives us—whether God is saying yes or no or wait—and to make the changes in ourselves that God asks of us.

Learn
I will refine them like silver and test them like gold.
They will call on my name and I will answer them;
I will say, "They are my people,"
and they will say, "The LORD is our God."

Zechariah 13:9

Unlearn
List the men in your prayer life and next to each name write something you have wanted God to change about him.

Prayer 5
Lord, show me how I need to change in each of the instances I have listed above. I am willing to be changed in whatever way you wish, and I need you to reveal to me, as I study and meditate on the Bible, pray, and talk with other Christians, what those changes you desire in me are and how I can change.

After you pray, note next to each item on the list the changes God reveals to you that you need to make.

Praying with Our Ears

*Our prayers are shaped by listening
to men and discerning God's will*

> Genuine listening means suspending memory, desire,
> and judgment—and, for a few moments at least, exist-
> ing for the other person.
> Michael P. Nichols, Ph.D., *The Lost Art of Listening*

The three years of Lonny's battle with cancer were
a lesson for his sister, Jeanne, and cousin Iris in listening to his needs and discerning what to pray.

Lonny was forty-seven when a routine insurance
checkup revealed cancer in his liver. Less than a year
before, Lonny, his sister, Jeanne, and his cousin Iris had
begun a weekly prayer telephone conference call to
pray for members of their huge extended family. Lonny
and Jeanne had always been very close, but neither had
been close to Iris before they discovered their common
faith and began their prayer conference calls. The three
of them lived in different parts of the country for most
of their adult lives, away from the city in which they
had been raised.

At first they prayed only for Lonny's healing. But as time passed, they began to understand that something supernatural was going on in Lonny's life, not just in his body.

Lonny's cancer was treated with chemotherapy. After the series of treatments was complete and pronounced successful in shrinking the egg-sized tumor to the size of a pea, he traveled nearly two thousand miles to visit Iris. It was only the second time they had ever seen each other in more than twenty years, except at family funerals or reunions. Their visit was an appointment made by God.

Lonny, who had been a star high school athlete, gone to college on a football scholarship, and weighed over two hundred pounds since he was fourteen years old, was still robust even after the chemo treatments. His bald head was appealing, even sexy. The only reminder that he wasn't in good health was the deep purple color of his fingernails.

But something inside Lonny had changed. What Iris heard as she listened to Lonny during their quiet four-day visit was a godly middle-aged husband and father searching for deeper meaning in his life, grappling with the challenge of true intimacy with God amidst the materialism, noise, and pace of daily family, work, and church life.

"Cancer hasn't brought me to my knees," Lonny chuckled. "I've been comfortable on my knees for many years," the Christian leader and godly household head continued humbly. Neither did Lonny doubt, question God, or falter in his faith.

But as Iris listened to Lonny ramble about his work, the kids, his beloved wife, and friends, she began to understand that Lonny had traveled so far to visit her because he needed to hear himself think aloud. "What has it changed about being on your knees?" Iris asked.

He cast her a quizzical glance. "You're asking how cancer has changed my prayers?"

"Mm-hmm," she mumbled sheepishly, wondering whether she had invaded his privacy.

Iris had felt uncomfortable when Lonny first asked if he could visit. It was so soon after his cancer treatments, and she had no idea how to entertain someone who was not strong enough to see the sights and do the town as a tourist, yet not sickly enough to be waited upon or cared for in some special way. Once she understood that all her telephone-prayer partner needed was a listening ear, she concentrated on making it easy for Lonny to express his thoughts and on reflecting back the meaning of what he said.

This wasn't easy for Iris. A mile-a-minute talker, she often finished others' sentences for them, and when she heard a comment tangential to something she had experienced, she'd turn the conversation to herself. But her big cousin fascinated her. He had sung in his church choir for years and had a mellifluous speaking voice. She found him easy to listen to, once she made up her mind to just listen. Even when he was silent for long, long minutes as he searched for words to express his feelings, she simply let silence reign.

She was in awe of God for Lonny's quick healing process and sensed that their unusual visit was God's request that she provide Lonny the inner space for the nonbodily healing God was doing. That inner space was created in part by Iris's listening.

"It *has* changed my prayers," he said after one of his long silences. "I used to talk to God. Now I'm straining, well, to hear him talk back to me. If that makes any sense..."

From listening to Lonny, Iris discerned that his prayer needs were for more than healing and renewed physical vigor, but during their visit, that is all she could specify.

When Lonny returned home to family, work, church, and his myriad Christian activities, her prayers were simply for his continued healing. But, their weekly conference-call prayers in the months after his visit subtly changed. She had different ears. She understood his pauses. When he grappled to articulate a thought or feeling, she could toss out a word or two to which he'd respond, "Yeah!" and then express himself more fully. Or, she could ask him a simple question as he rambled on, testing his own thoughts, and he'd hone in and declare clearly *the* thought or *the* feeling he had found so hard to identify in himself and express. It was like jump-starting a car.

Iris continued to feel a lingering need to pray for something beyond Lonny's healing, but she remained unable to identify what it was.

The next year Lonny was diagnosed with a virulent cancer in his lymph system and several tumors in other parts of his body. It was a spiritual blow. The doctors recommended a bone marrow transplant, saying he would otherwise die quickly, but they projected only a 50 percent chance of survival from the transplant. Lonny visited several individuals who had had successful bone-marrow operations and decided from their pitiful conditions that "survival" was not for him. He wanted to *live*. Lonny declined medical treatment and chose instead to rely on prayer and to radically alter his diet and lifestyle.

It was only then that Iris began to discern the prayer need: for God to reveal the *purpose* of the cancer in Lonny's life.

Four months after ignoring the stringent objections of his doctors for declining medical treatment and making drastic dietary and lifestyle changes, Lonny's doctor evaluated his tests and commented, "There is no scientific explanation for why you are doing so well."

A season later, Lonny attended the funeral of a seventeen-year-old, one of six other patients who had been diagnosed at the same time as Lonny. Of the seven in their patient group, only Lonny remained alive, and his life was normal, though his frame, now at a "mere" 205 pounds, was, he said, a sliver of his old body. As Iris listened to Lonny talk about the funeral, she clearly discerned that she needed to pray, "Reveal what you want Lonny to get from this cancer experience, Lord."

Lonny's own cry to God was for direction. God had moved miraculously in his healing, opening doors for him to make huge adjustments in his lifestyle—regarding stress, work, diet, and exercise—without harmful financial effects on his family. Yet healing wasn't enough in itself. "If God wants me to live, what am I to live to *do?*" seemed to be Lonny's dilemma as he sadly described attending the teenager's funeral to Iris. As she listened and discerned, she committed to also pray for God's direction in Lonny's life.

The next fall Lonny, a college grad with two dozen years of professional management experience, enrolled in a Bible college that emphasized home and foreign missionary work.

That winter, after years of experiments, a new intravenous, nonsurgical treatment was approved for the type of cancer still present, but not advancing, in Lonny's body. The treatment, given on an outpatient basis with few side effects, eliminated all but the last few shrinking vestiges of the cancer. Lonny felt better than he had in years. Even before the confirming tests, he knew the treatment was working.

As he talked about going back to work, the natural course was for Lonny to return to his well-paid, high-stress managerial position, but he and Iris knew that was not the supernatural course. His conversation turned more and more to missions. Iris discerned that God allowed Lonny's illness to redirect his life, and her quiet prayer for this man was for God to provide him specific new direction.

———◼———

Through listening and discerning, we discover the prayer issues God wants us to raise on a man's behalf. Before we look for the words to articulate our thoughts and feelings to God, we must listen. We must listen, so men will talk to us. We have to earn their trust. That also means never using their self-revelations to make judgments or as ammunition when we are hurt or mad. By listening, we can discern their prayer needs and pray God's will for them.

It is good to pray for our perceived needs of the men in our lives and our concerns and desires for them. It is even more powerful to pray *along with* them for their stated needs and to pray in harmony with what we discern is God's will for them.

Voice this simple prayer:

Prayer 6
Lord, show me how to pray for _____.
Help me not to judge his needs, but teach me how to listen to his concerns and to discern what you want me to pray for on his behalf. Show me how to pray in harmony with your will and pray with respect for the issues about which he has expressed concern.

If you believe the man you are praying for has not told you what specifically to pray on his behalf, pray the above prayer and note where you will learn those specifics—from listening to him and from discerning God's will.

This listening-discerning approach to prayer applies the principle of praying "in agreement" based on Matthew 18:18–19: "Whatever you bind on earth will be bound in heaven, and whatever you loose on earth will be loosed in heaven.... If two of you on earth agree about anything you ask for, it will be done for you by my Father in heaven." Prayer itself is powerful. Praying with another is even more powerful. According to these words from Jesus' ministry, making our prayers the same as those of the men we are praying for is stronger than praying our own petitions for him and stronger than his own prayers for himself.

We also want to pray in agreement with God so that what we "bind on earth" can "be bound in heaven." Our prayers open the way for God to act. He is relying on us to allow the spiritual to become material. We create a pathway for God's intentions to be given human energy. Therefore, we want our prayers to parallel God's will. Discerning what God wants you to pray produces even more dynamic prayer than what you and the man could pray together.

Ecclesiastes states the obvious truth of strength in numbers simply and succinctly: "Though one may be overpowered, two can defend themselves" (4:12). But this verse also takes the principle a step further, into the spiritual realm: "A cord of three strands is not quickly broken" (4:12). That third strand is God.

To pray in agreement with the man and with God, we must listen. "He who has ears, let him hear" (Matthew 11:15).

Listening So Men Will Talk

One of the universally recognized differences between men and women is their communication styles. That women talk and men don't is an overstated stereotype, but it contains a lot of truth. Some Christians believe this difference is inherent in our creation; other Christians hold that it is part of our fallen nature. For the purpose of praying for the men in our lives, it is not important to ponder the roots or even the truth of this apparent difference.

It *is* important, however, to understand that humans, regardless of gender, respond to active, empathic listening. The most powerful intercessors are not great orators, they are great listeners. If we learn dynamic listening skills and view listening as part of the call to prayer, the men in our life will talk with us about their concerns.

Praying with our ears means listening to the men in our lives so we hear the concerns God desires to address. Most of us pray about what *we* think God should address. Sometimes we believe God has "shown" us what we should pray. That belief is presumptuous. It is more likely that the prayer needs of the man we are praying for are first made apparent to him. The challenge is opening communication, getting him to discover and explore what God is saying to him and to share that openly with us.

In order for others to talk to us so we can pray about their real needs, we must be intercessory listeners. Our first step toward intercessory listening is to accept "otherness"—that others have the God-given right to be, think, behave, talk, and live differently than us. We cannot judge and intercede at the same time. We cannot judge and listen at the same time. If we want the truth from our men, we must make it easy for them to plumb their inner depths to discover their own truths and then make it safe for them to tell us that truth. When we as women say men don't talk, we overlook the planks in our own eyes (Matthew 7:3–5). We fail to create a nonjudgmental atmosphere where men can open up to us.

Here is a brief list of ways we keep the men in our lives from talking and some starters for developing prayer-attuned hearing:

Pressuring Him to Open Up

Instead of pressuring him to open up, accept that he does not want to talk and let him know you understand that he doesn't want to say anything. Do so gently without becoming intense. Give him your blessing on keeping his thoughts and feelings to himself. For example, you could say, "I really believe God's Word when it says, there's a time to be silent (Ecclesiastes 3:7). Just know I'm here for you."

Then simply be with him. Remain present or available and allow the situation to be relaxed. Learn to be comfortable with him in silence. This helps end the cat-and-mouse game women often play to get men to talk. If this is a pattern with you and your husband, you and your teenager, you and your dad, you and any man, you can pray for him most effectively if you change the paradigm. Learn to feel safe with him in silence. It can be scary at first, but over time, silences between two people become shared peace. Force yourself *not* to make small talk and just *be*. This does not mean be passive. The longer you practice being in the same place with him and not forcing conversation, the more you will understand the many ways we communicate nonverbally and the less uncomfortable you will become. It may take a long time to break a well-established pattern of forced conversation, but once it is broken, real expression and genuine listening can begin.

People who don't open up are sometimes avoiding hurt. Examine whether you have

- used something he said against him;
- typecast, judged, condemned, or blamed him because of something he revealed to you in a conversation;
- made him feel powerless because of something he said;

- overreacted emotionally or physically to his words;
- repeated to others something he shared; or
- taken his words personally.

You may need to seek forgiveness and take the long road of rebuilding trust before you can expect him to open up to you.

Men also may not talk because they don't expect to be listened to. They think, *Why bother to dig deep and find words for my thoughts and feelings, when she won't really listen to me anyway?* If we have interrupted, argued, or criticized him a lot, *we* might feel he doesn't talk, but he might feel we don't listen. Saying we want to listen won't change the situation. Even learning listening "techniques" won't completely change it. Cultivating a God-given, selfless caring that makes us really want to understand him in order to bring his prayer needs before God *will* change things. We cannot change a withholder. We can change ourselves, however, and with God's help, we can become irresistible listeners. Remember that God is going to answer our prayers for our men by changing us.

Some men by nature *don't* dig deep. They are simple at heart. People have various depths psychologically, and if you are a "deep" woman praying for a "simple" man, you will need to accept that he may never open up by your definition of being open. Our culture over-glorifies examining and sharing our thoughts and feelings. Men who are not so complex or who don't overanalyze everything are often peaceful and restful to be around. And, again, there are many other ways of communicating besides talking. Let him be.

Feeling We Need to Do Something

Our feelings are communicated even when we don't speak. While we're "listening" to the men we want to pray for, we're taking mental notes so as soon as we finish listening to what they say, we can defend ourselves, agree or disagree, solve the problem, correct them, change their thinking, help them make their point, and so on.

Instead, prayer-attuned hearing means we unhinge our feelings. We simply make ourselves an open receptacle for whatever our men say. We become completely absorbed in receiving their meanings. As they talk, our response is, "Mm-hmm" and "I see." Our minds are 100 percent focused on understanding.

Think of it as a game. Rather than a tennis game, a volley back and forth, in this prayerful-listening game, the men have baseballs and we have mitts. They only throw, and we only catch. Ball after ball is thrown, and our task is to run after and catch each one, no matter how difficult it is. We don't throw it back or bat it. We simply do our best to catch and examine the balls being thrown. We simply listen.

Reacting Emotionally

Instead of letting our men's words "push our buttons," we choose not to react right now. Now is the time to listen. We might decide to react at another time, a later time, but for right now we concentrate on hearing and understanding.

Self-control is a fruit of God's Spirit (Galatians 5:23), and it is possible to listen without automatically responding, without overreacting. Even when what they say feels like criticism, we can listen without an emotional reaction. The key is to concentrate on listening more intently. If necessary, take out a notepad or journal and write down what he says. "I really want to understand what you're saying, and I know I'll have a hard time remembering, so I'm jotting it down. Okay?"

At the root of our emotional reactions is the desire to control. In God's order, the only person you can control is yourself. We may have God-given authority over others, but authority is not control. In fact, the obligation to listen comes with authority. "Shut up." "Don't you speak to me that way!" "I won't hear another word of this kind of talk." Such are the emotional reactions that sometimes prevent us from hearing real prayer needs. By listening we can sift through a disrespectful tone, unappealing language, and even insults, rather than react to them, which may be necessary to discover and really hear the nuggets of true feelings, thoughts, and needs. We can then lift those to God in prayer. Let go of your need to control what he says, and let God teach you to listen, even when what you hear hurts.

Emotionalism also comes from anxiety and feeling like we *don't* have control of a situation. Reminding ourselves that God is in charge allows us to listen calmly even in conversations that would formerly have enraged us. Listening means giving up the right to seek control. As Christians we understand that we are giving our desires for control to God, not to other people. We are hearing others fully, so when we go to God in prayer, we have received all the information that God has provided. Yielding control of a matter to God in prayer does not mean snatching control back from God in conversation.

Sometimes we women don't believe we are coming across as emotionally as men perceive us to be. For example, we feel we are "chatting" when men might hear us "shrilling." It is a good idea, in general, always to turn our emotions down a notch or two when we want to really listen. Even if you don't feel you are reacting emotionally, use the man's sense of relaxation as a mirror, and err on the side of lowering nonverbal communication—sighs, raised eyebrows, hand gestures, mouth puckering, and so forth.

We naturally have high emotions about some issues. Those are often the very things we are praying about. Those same concerns are ones for which we need to resist the urge to react emotionally and instead listen. With God's help, we can suspend those emotions to listen well. That may mean suspending, for this occasion, very legitimate and appropriate reactions. Now is a time solely for listening. It is time devoted to forgoing our own emotions and thoughts, no matter how valid, and letting God use us to care more deeply about hearing and understanding what the men we are praying for are saying.

Not Acknowledging or Seeking to Understand What He Is Saying

Instead of formulating a response to what your man says, be genuinely interested in entering into his experience. The goal is to be receptive, rather than responsive. Desire to see the world as he sees it, to be in tune with his inner self. Michael P. Nichols, in *The Lost Art of Listening*, writes, "Listening has not one but two purposes: taking in information and bearing witness to another's expression." It is part literal, hearing what is said, and part intuition, an inner sensing.

We acknowledge our men and seek or show understanding when we ask questions for clarification and encourage elaboration. As they talk, our responses are "Really?" "So you're saying (rephrase his words into our own words)..." "Uh-huh, explain that some more." We might also make intuitive guesses to elicit further talk, for example, "It sounds like you were feeling ..."

Even if his "facts" are wrong, don't interrupt. Feelings *are* facts to him. Praying with ears means listening to how he perceives and sees things, even if to him blue is orange and two plus two equals five.

Conversing Because We're Needy

Again, rather than really wanting to hear what they have to say, we often attempt to butter men up, flatter them, or say things that will push their buttons because we want conversations about issues due to our own needs. We are not genuinely seeking to hear their thoughts and feelings; we only want to discuss things or get them out into the open. This is not the same as listening.

Even a need as sacred as bringing a matter to God in prayer does not justify conversation for our own sakes. The men we are praying for will likely view such attempts at conversation as bogus. There is no substitute for cultivating in ourselves a genuine desire to hear and understand their points of view. We must be prepared and God-equipped to really listen.

Hearing What We Want to Hear

Instead of hearing our men's thoughts and feelings, we women often hear what we think they said the last time, what we hope they're saying, or what they've said over and over for years. We must listen for their *meaning*. The words might indeed be the same, but with new God-given hearing, we discover that we never really "heard," we never understood the meaning of those words before.

If what he says sounds like you've heard it before, will yourself to hear it, as if, for the first time. Listen without any history—your own or his. Listen as God listens to you. God has forgiven you, has put your sins as far as the east is from the west, has made you a new creation with your old self gone. God listens to you with fresh mercy each time you pray. Extend that kind of listening. Hear what he says without any preconceived notions.

In this prayer-attuned hearing, we actually forget ourselves in the process of listening.

Prayer 7

Lord, give me ears to hear _____'s words, as well as his thoughts and feelings underneath the words.

Move me out of the way of _____'s expressing himself. Replace my reactions with the empathy of Jesus to what he says and how he says it.

Lord, please identify in me the habits that prevent _____ from opening up to me and let your Spirit in me replace them with new ways that will make me an irresistible listener.

Discernment

Even with the best human communication, not everything can be known. Even with our best listening, we need God's Spirit to enable us to discern the unspeakable, to discover the truths that hover in silences, to read actions and decipher doings.

Discernment is the spiritual equivalent of our senses. Just as hearing is a bodily sense—a way we take in physical information—discernment is how we take in spiritual data.

> The man without the Spirit does not accept the things that come from the Spirit of God, for they are foolishness to him, and he cannot understand them, because they are spiritually discerned.
>
> 1 Corinthians 2:14

Prayer is connecting with God. Because God is Spirit (John 4:24), prayer is a human-Spirit connection, a supernatural connection. We're natural and God is super. God allows us to pray with more than what we can receive naturally through our senses; he gives us discernment. Hearing is a natural sense. Discernment is a spiritual quality.

Discernment allows us to see past surfaces. It is a spiritual insight that allows us to perceive on a level that is sharper than our senses and is not motivated by our human inclinations. It is developed in a spiritual context:

> And this is my *prayer*: that your *love* may abound more and more in knowledge and depth of insight, so that you may be able to discern what is best.
>
> Philippians 1:9–10 (emphasis added)

Just as we can become better listeners, Christians can also acquire God-given discernment. We can receive it by asking for it in prayer that is motivated by love (James 4:3).

God provides discernment so we will know God's will and pray in harmony with it. To pray for the men in our lives in agreement with the man and with God, we must listen to the man and discern what God wants us to perceive.

Prayer 8

Lord, you are the great hearer of prayer and discerner of thoughts. Give me abounding love for _____ as a fruit of your Spirit. With that spirit of love, give me the gift of discernment so I will be able to pray what is pleasing to you, to pray for your perfect will on his behalf, and to operate in harmony with my prayers.

Learn
The purposes of a man's heart are deep waters,
but a [wo]man of understanding draws them out.
Proverbs 20:5

Unlearn
List the men in your prayer life and next to each
name write something you have done that might
have prevented him from opening up to you.

1.

2.

3.

4.

5.

Prayer 9

Lord, show me what to say or not say in each
of the instances I have listed above, so I can genuinely hear the true needs for prayer. Reveal to
me, through your gift of discernment, what you
desire as my prayers for each of these men.

After you pray, note next to each item on the list
what you will say or not say in each instance the
next time it occurs.

Praying for Him When He Can't Pray for Himself

An assignment from God to pray on his behalf

Somebody prayed for me,
had me on their mind;
took the time
and prayed for me.
I'm so glad they prayed,
I'm so glad they prayed,
I'm so glad they prayed for me.
  Traditional song in the African American church

God appoints an unlikely intercessor in this Christian couple's troubled love story.

"There's a cute girl working in the lawyer's office at the strip mall," Bobby's father said to him.

When Ursula opened the door to the lawyer's office and Bobby saw her for the first time, he said, "You *are* a beaut!" Ursula had rolled her beautiful eyes and simply closed the door. So began Bobby's six-year pursuit of Ursula.

An acknowledged backslid Christian, Bobby wanted a good time and knew how to win a woman. He sent Ursula flowers. He paid respectful visits to her home. He called. He persisted, even riding his bike miles to her house when his car broke down.

A newly converted Christian, Ursula wanted nothing to do with Bobby's games. She had played them before she gave her life to Christ, and her own experience had taught her that only God's Spirit could change a man like him. She made it clear to Bobby that since he was not living a godly life, they could only be casual friends. Bobby heard Ursula's words as coy retreats, encouraging him to stronger pursuit.

So, Bobby began going to church. He had made a heartfelt commitment to God through Christ when he was a boy, but the lures of the teenage world had drawn him away from God. In his early twenties, following Ursula's scent, he suddenly found himself back in touch with God. "I've never denied the truth of God," he told Ursula. "Yes, I have a personal relationship with God," he said truthfully, when she queried him, and reminded her, "I *am* going to church with you."

"It's not just about church, Bobby!"

"Hey, I believe in God, okay? I do *not* believe in all those party-killing rules!" he added, only half joking. "I'm just not ready to be into it as deep and heavy as you, Ursula."

To Bobby, it didn't take *all that*—abstinence, sobriety, monogamy—to be a Christian. He was a Christian! He was just a man—a man in his early twenties who wanted to have a good time like everyone else. Most of those old-timers in the church had probably done the same thing when they were young. He liked drinking, smoking weed, committing any crimes he could get away with, and especially laying up with women. He imagined the day he'd have Ursula. Those hard-to-get ones were the sweetest. He settled for "friendship" with Ursula, biding his time. After all, she was really great to talk with and to be around. There were always other women around to satisfy his needs as a man. Being back in church was all right too. It felt good to be back in contact with God. Sometimes when Bobby was all by himself, he prayed—the Lord's Prayer, the Twenty-third Psalm. He even caught himself reciting "Now I lay me down to sleep" one night as he nodded off high from some wicked weed.

Having dropped out of high school, then earning his GED and enrolling in community college before he met Ursula, Bobby transferred to a local university, earned his degree, and headed off to a prestigious graduate school. Their friendship continued and to his continued amazement, Ursula had still not given him any sex.

When Bobby left their small city for one of the largest cities in the nation, he knew he had arrived. Here were women of every variety, the best drugs routinely available, nonstop parties, all in a sophisticated atmosphere of anonymity and live-and-let-live attitudes. Bobby slid into this large world with ease, rising to the top of his grad school class academically and winning popularity as a chief partyer and player.

As he made his transition to grad school life in the big city, Bobby found himself missing church. He missed Ursula too, but that feeling was more easily drowned out by the constant parade of women. Here, a man didn't even have to pursue. Often the women were the aggressors, wanting the same kind of just-keep-it-physical relationship he liked. But that church feeling was harder to make go away. There was no substitute for it. When he wasn't too hung over, busy with his studies, or still with the previous night's babe, he visited churches on Sundays in the late morning. He discovered a nondenominational megachurch whose pastor preached in a style that was so academic that Bobby began to remember and reflect on sermons and Scripture long after the emotive messages had passed. He liked the size of the church because he could remain invisible. More and more the pastor's teachings made him think— about the meaning of life, about God, about himself. He began attending regularly, and at the same time, the thrills of his daily life started to feel like more of the same.

It was always good to talk to Ursula back home.

"Hey, Bobby, what a surprise to hear from you. How *are* you?" He could tell from her voice that his success had pushed him up a notch with Ursula.

"It's all good. You?"

"Well, I'm teaching Sunday school now, working with the teenage girls in the church."

"Still churching," he said flatly. Now, *she* had just gone up another notch.

"Of course. It's a challenge, but I love the teens. Oh, and I left the law office and got a job working for a Christian organization. It even pays more. God is amazing."

"You're even deeper in it now; your job's about church too."

"It's a Christian publication, not a church, Bobby. And guess what? I'm about to enroll in grad school, like you."

Nobody outside of their area had ever heard of the local university to which she had been offered a full scholarship. He teased, "What are you taking?

No, let me guess—religion, or one of those helping profession degrees that never made anybody rich or famous?"

After earning his master's degree, and making a fabulous start on his career, Bobby rededicated his life to the Lord. An opportunity arose for Bobby to cofacilitate a small neighborhood Bible study group. He was flattered and agreed, but said he would miss many meetings due to travel as he made a name for himself in his field.

Bobby's gifts of spiritual knowledge and for teaching the Bible blossomed immediately, stunning others and even himself. From there, in his own words, he "completely sold out for the Lord." Ursula, who had grown to love Bobby over the years, but held back because of his lifestyle, now began to express her feelings for him. Soon after, he decided to marry Ursula and move her to the city.

Right away their problems began, and the critical need for intercessory prayer arose. Claudette, an older woman in the neighborhood Bible study Bobby helped lead, had been praying casually for Bobby since the group began. It was evident to her that God was working powerfully in and through Bobby.

While Bobby and Ursula had always stayed in contact by telephone and he visited her while home on vacations, she had not once, during his years in the big city, visited him. In fact, Ursula had never even been on an airplane. Now, Bobby invited her to visit and she accepted.

Claudette was delighted when Bobby shared with her his plans to give Ursula a ring on her first visit to the city, impressed with their commitment to sexual purity during their courtship, and honored that he wanted Ursula to stay with her during the visit.

Ursula arrived at the older woman's home flush from the excitement of her first flight and, unable to answer audibly when Claudette greeted her with the question, "Did you accept?" excitedly flashed the large diamond engagement ring on her finger.

Three tumultuous months later when Bobby asked Ursula to return the ring, the older woman felt a deep personal calling to continue to pray for their relationship. At first she prayed in agreement with Bobby, sure that he and Ursula would overcome the causes of their breakup—numerous disagreements over practical matters involving their wedding and conflicts arising from the need to combine two very different styles of life. Hurt and confused, Bobby seemed comforted by her prayers.

But within months after the engagement was broken off, Bobby began to confide in Claudette his interests in other women. He did consider only Christian women, one at a time, and set boundaries for himself that precluded sexual intercourse. Bobby spoke of Ursula in the past tense. When the older woman mentioned to Bobby that she was still praying for him and Ursula to marry, he frankly asked her to stop. "It's over between Ursula and me," he said. "We're still friends, but we're never getting married. I just don't feel that way for her anymore. I've moved on." Every few months, a new name dropped into his conversations with Claudette—some beautiful young woman at church, some attractive woman in a Christian organization, an alluring Christian he had met through his work. Something still compelled Claudette to continue to pray for him and Ursula.

Eventually Bobby and Ursula's friends and even their families, who had grown to love the espoused as one of their own, stopped praying for them to be reunited. It wasn't God's will, they supposed. They worked at helping the two grieve their long friendship and broken engagement, and get on with their separate lives. But more than ever Claudette felt the call to pray for their relationship, and she set about that task in earnest. "God bring Bobby and Ursula back together" was her repeated, unwavering prayer over the months.

After a while Bobby and Ursula became a thing of the past. Their names weren't mentioned in unison anymore. Claudette felt a little silly asking

God for something that was so obviously a closed door. She didn't want to seem as if she weren't minding her own business, so she prayed for Bobby and Ursula's marriage in her solitude with God and in her confidential prayer circle.

Then an exotically beautiful young woman joined their Bible group. She had been attending church off and on for several years, had made a confession of faith, and was soon to be baptized. The young woman and Bobby discovered they worked in the same field. They were also both avid golfers. She invited Bobby for a game and their relationship began on the greens. It escalated quickly to "more than just friends" as the young woman shared with Claudette, who listened and, in secret, steadfastly prayed for Bobby and Ursula's relationship.

When news spread that Bobby had eloped, most of his friends laughed and asked, "With whom?" It was almost a year, to the day, after he and Ursula had broken off their engagement. When the glowing newlyweds—Bobby and Ursula—returned, they invited Claudette out to dinner to thank her for her prayers. One of her "confidential" prayer circle partners had shared with Bobby that the older woman had continued to pray for them the entire year.

"You and Ursula's mom were the only two people who kept praying for us. *We* stopped praying for us to get back together!" Bobby said. "I never thought I'd hear myself say something like this," he continued, "but, while I was jogging one day, it was like a dam broke. I knew beyond a doubt that I needed to be in *God's* will. I prayed about Urz and me in a way I had never been able to before. All the reasons I broke the marriage off became obstacles that we could handle if I chose to live in God's will. God's will became my focus, not what kind of wedding or lifestyle she wanted, not what I dreamed of in a wife, but what I knew was God's will. Thank you, Claudette. God really used your prayers."

Claudette had to hold back tears. She could imagine the powerful work God would do through this dynamic Christian couple, and she was convinced even more of the effectiveness of prayer to break strongholds that might prevent God's purposes from being accomplished.

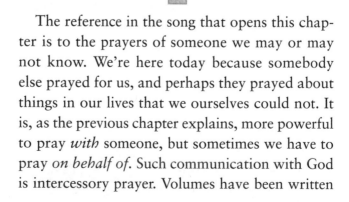

The reference in the song that opens this chapter is to the prayers of someone we may or may not know. We're here today because somebody else prayed for us, and perhaps they prayed about things in our lives that we ourselves could not. It is, as the previous chapter explains, more powerful to pray *with* someone, but sometimes we have to pray *on behalf of*. Such communication with God is intercessory prayer. Volumes have been written on it, so I will bring out only a few points for those who are praying especially for men. Start with the following deceptively simple words:

> **Prayer 10**
> Lord, prepare me to be an intercessor for _____. Thank you for giving me the privilege of being one small connector between your plans for him and the outworking of those plans.

Intercession Is a Calling

Intercessory prayer is often a deeply-felt knowing, a calling. Recently, I experienced this in our church's midweek prayer gathering. A patient who needed a heart transplant came and placed himself at the altar. He was a category D candidate for a transplant, meaning A, B, and C were before him; he was way down the list. When he came to prayer service that night, my spirit picked up on his need, and I began to pray mightily for God to find a person whose organs were compatible with his and for him to get a heart donor. Within twenty-four hours he went from category D up to category A. By the end of the following day—before forty-eight hours had passed—he was in surgery. He had a successful heart transplant. I already believed in the power of intercessory prayer, and yet my faith was reaffirmed by this miraculous situation. I assure you: interceding in prayer is powerful.

As a pastor, I am familiar and comfortable with intercessory prayer. It is an important role for church leaders. Although you may not be at ease in that role, you can be a crucial intercessor in the lives of the men you know.

In the story of Bobby and Ursula, Claudette felt compelled to continue to pray for them, although it appeared pointless and her prayers were expressly unimportant to Bobby. Prayer is what intercessors feel *led* to do, something they *must* do. Intercessors pray as an assignment from God. The calling is often described as a continuing faint, yet very pronounced, irresistible urge to pray on someone's behalf.

If you are wondering whether or not God has called you to intercede for the man you are praying for, the answer is yes. If you are feeling the urge to pray for him, you are responding to God. Whenever those of us who believe Jesus is Lord pray, it is a response to God (Jeremiah 31:3 and John 6:44).

The call to intercession can feel lonely. On our knees with our face to the ground, sitting quietly in our favorite chair, in the pew or folding seat at church, the process of going to God again and again on behalf of our brothers, husbands, fathers, sons, or friends can feel totally solitary. It can feel as if you are the only one praying, and that feeling of isolation can make even the best prayer warriors want to quit. But don't! Often, as in the case of Bobby and Ursula where Claudette only learned later that Ursula's mother had also continued to pray, we eventually discover that someone else who we don't even know was praying the same thing. We learn we were praying in agreement all along. Be encouraged. Scripture reminds us that God always has a remnant, a small piece of leftover fabric. At least two threads—a weft and a warp—always compose a remnant.

Intercession vs. Interference

God has a plan to fulfill in the man you are praying for. As an intercessor, you are the midwife of God's plan for him.

Effective intercessory prayer means letting go of your plan for the man and praying for God's plan. A midwife has no tie to the baby; the baby belongs to the mom and dad, no matter how hard the helpers worked to deliver it. Intercessors understand their role, almost instinctively. In fact, they often have no plan and no attachment to a specific outcome. They frequently question their own interest and motives and approach God wondering, *Why am I praying about this? This is not my concern. Why am I including him in my prayers?*

Claudette, the older woman in the story above, remarked in her prayer circle that "there's a thin line between ministry and meddling." Careful not to interfere, she prayed out of a powerful urge that turned out to be from God, but while praying, she still had to fight the feeling that the matter was none of her business. As Bobby and Ursula's friend, she accepted their choice to move on with their separate lives. As an intercessor, appointed by God, she continued to pray for them.

Because intercessory prayer is an assignment from God to act as a conduit, a go-between, a connector between God and the man we are praying for, we can choose whether or not to answer God's call to intercession. We can accept the assignment to intercede or ignore it. But, we do not choose *what* we pray for as intercessors.

Sometimes the purpose and specifics of the prayers that need to be offered are only revealed over time. Other times the exact prayers to be uttered are provided by the Holy Spirit.

> We do not know what we ought to pray for, but the Spirit himself intercedes for us with groans that words cannot express. And he who searches our hearts knows the mind of the Spirit, because the Spirit intercedes for the saints in accordance with God's will.

> Romans 8:26–27

In intercession, God calls us to pray on behalf of others and to pray God's will. This may involve talking with God about intimate matters. In the process, we may discern issues that are private. It is best to keep such matters confidential.

Intercessors are called to pray so God can work. The work is not ours to do. Prayer is our role. Interfering, confronting, and sharing information, whether gleaned from our conversations with God or others, are not part of intercession. Intercession begins and ends with prayer.

Prayer 11

Lord Jesus, I submit myself to you, empty of motives and plans for _____. Show me what you want me to pray on his behalf. And until I am confident I have heard from you, Lord, I pray simply that your plans for him become his reality.

Intercession Breaks Through

Often the reason we cannot pray with or in agreement with a man is because something is preventing him from optimal communication with God. He may be blocked, unable to discern God's will for him, and your prayers may be necessary to remove what is preventing his own direct communication with God.

Is something hindering his prayers or keeping him from living a godly life (Hebrews 12:1)? Are there ideologies or errors in his thinking that are causing negative effects (2 Corinthians 10:5)? Does he make a practice of doing something displeasing to God (John 8:34)?

In Bobby's case, his past dealings with women hindered him in that critical engagement stage when couples must handle the real issues of building a life together. Ideas shaped by his ungodly relationships and associations had taken a strong hold in his thinking. He stopped praying. But God called intercessors, and there was a breakthrough.

In chapter 4, the listening-discerning approach to prayer emphasized the principle of praying "in agreement"—making your prayers the same as those of the man you are praying for—based on Matthew 18:18–19: "Whatever you bind on earth will be bound in heaven, and whatever you loose on earth will be loosed in heaven. . . . If two of you on earth agree about anything you ask for, it will be done for you by my Father in heaven."

In instances where the man's own prayers are hindered, your prayers on his behalf might need to be that those hindrances be bound and the man be loosed from those very specific concerns. God has promised to parallel us in the spiritual realm. For example, Claudette may have prayed that the attitudes Bobby formed in his ungodly relationships not bind him in his relationship with Ursula, that his mind would be loosed from those ideas, and that he be free to seek God's will regarding his relationship with Ursula. Claudette prayed; soon Bobby was able to pray again. Bobby's decision to marry Ursula after their long breakup came, he said, through prayer. As Bobby sought God's direction for his life in general, God softened Bobby's heart toward her and revealed to Bobby that his destiny and Ursula's were intertwined. A stronghold had been broken.

A hindrance that slows or distracts a man, an ideological stronghold that confuses him or stunts his growth, a habitual practice that prevents him from being the person he truly is or even seriously damages him—each of these challenges can be faced in intercessory prayer. Prayer is the military maneuver of spiritual warfare. The well-known passage in Ephesians 6:11–18 names Scripture as the one offensive weapon in spiritual battles and cites prayer as the only offensive *action*. The others are defensive ones involving spiritual armor. Intercessory prayer that incorporates Scripture is powerful when breakthroughs are needed.

Intercessory Warfare: Praying the Scriptures

There are excellent books available on how to pray the Scriptures, inserting your man's name in the scriptural context. My approach is a bit different. Rather than starting with a passage of Scripture, we begin by seeking God in prayer and asking *him* to reveal the appropriate Scripture. "Things that come from the Spirit of God ... are spiritually discerned" (1 Corinthians 2:14).

In many cases we know only the effects, not the causes of the issues hindering the man for whom we're praying. Asking God to give us the Scripture that needs to be prayed takes full benefit of the Spirit. It does not rely on our five senses and our always-imperfect discernment for information from which to choose what we think is an appropriate passage of Scripture.

This method of praying the Scriptures is for women of the Word, those who read the Bible regularly and widely. If you consistently spend time in the Bible and study it for application to your life and for deeper meanings, you will likely experience breakthroughs when you ask our Lord to reveal, by the Holy Spirit, the Scripture for the man you are concerned about.

After you pray for the Scripture, you may recognize the verse or passage God is giving you in a number of ways. For some, a Scripture just comes to mind. Others receive it in the form of congruencies. For example, a passage from a Sunday sermon keeps turning over in your mind. It doesn't obviously apply to the man you are praying for, but yet the unlikely connection lingers in your mind. On Monday, a Christian coworker, who knows nothing of the sermon at your church, mentions the passage. You pray and God confirms by giving you a peace that is stronger than your mental powers (Philippians 4:7) that this is the Scripture you are to pray.

Once God has given you the Scripture, read it in as many translations of the Bible as you can. Prayerfully, write out its meaning in *your own words,* inserting your man's name where appropriate. Then meditate on what you have written. Quietly, say it over and over, until you have memorized it naturally, without treating it as a memorization exercise. The goal is to retain the *meaning,* not the exact words. If you're poetic, recite it as verse; if you're musical, hum it to a tune you love, or make it into a song. Let it become part of your permanent memory, on the tip of your tongue, always ready at the back of your mind. It sounds cliché, but these are ways to grasp the practical aspects of meditation and help you meditate in today's busy lifestyles.

Finally, in your quiet time with God, pray the Scripture. Open yourself to the answers God provides you, in the form of other Scriptures to pray, in changes in you, and in perceptible differences in the man for whom you're praying.

Prayer 12

Lord Jesus, you said that whatever we bind on earth will be bound in heaven, and whatever we loose on earth will be loosed in heaven. With this prayer, I bind _____ in _____'s life. And, Lord, I loose _____ to be free to relate to you directly in prayer on his own behalf.

Learn

I urge, then, first of all, that requests, prayers, intercession and thanksgiving be made for everyone.

1 Timothy 2:1

Unlearn

Using the same list of the men in your prayer life from chapter 2, note something you have done that might seem to him or others as interfering.

Prayer 13

Lord Jesus, help me to decrease as you increase.

6

Man-Sized Prayers in No Time

Big needs, little me, no time

Our life comes to us moment by moment. One moment disappears before the next comes along: and there is room for very little in each. That is what Time is like. . . .

Almost certainly God is not in Time. His life does not consist of moments following one another.

C. S. Lewis, *Mere Christianity*

God showed Lindsay that the man-sized prayers she needed to pray for five urban teenage boys in her Sunday school class didn't require any more time and that God had already given her what *was* required for those prayers.

Lindsay closed the door of the Sunday school class-room and sat down and cried. She knew the Lord would see her through, but she needed a good cry before she could venture down the corridor to the 11:00 A.M. worship service.

It was her second week teaching the ninth, tenth, and eleventh grade class. She had been reassigned mid-semester after the regular team of teachers—a man and woman who had years of experience working with teenagers—decided not to continue. She didn't know exactly why. She loved teaching the twenty-something Sunday school class; the previous year's class had been her first teaching assignment in her new church home. It had gone very well, and she had looked forward to returning to that age group.

But the previous week Norma, the Sunday school superintendent, had asked, "Lindsay, would you take the senior high class? We really need you there. The twenties can be a self-directed class."

The unruly, disrespectful teens seemed determined to take out on her their frustration that their parents made them come to church. During the first class, she had warned them about their behavior repeatedly and led them in a discussion of the rules of fellowship.

This second class, the direct, personal verbal rebellion stunned and hurt her. Before she could think, she had sent five students out of the class. They were not to return until they committed themselves to abide by the fellowship rules.

Lindsay had loved church since she was a child. She had always found pleasure in the company of church folk, thrived on preaching, was stimulated by Bible study, and enjoyed worshiping and singing. Even the walk to and from church were part of what made Sunday her favorite day of the week. Now going to church meant lying awake with dread on Saturday night, then dragging out of bed, only to worry whether what she chose to wear would draw ridicule from those smart-mouths, who came to church in baggy pants (boys) and skin-tight spandex (girls).

This morning she had forced herself to get up, gathered the show-and-tell—Christian pop music and other paraphernalia the teen teaching guides said were necessary to interest today's teens in God—and frantically hailed a cab. These brats had robbed her joy.

She wiped her eyes and pulled herself together. As she headed to the sanctuary, she wondered what the repercussions would be. Those expelled were kids of deacons, elders, ushers, and others active in the church. They had left the classroom with airs that they were special and knew it. She uttered a prayer for God's help and dashed into the service.

The next Sunday, Norma greeted her with a gentle admonishment, "Show more love and the kids will love you." As if reading her mind, Norma added, "You *could* quit; you *could* give up on the Lord."

Lindsay gritted her teeth and thought about the two recently-resigned teachers. She pursed her lips into her churchy smile, which hid her anger that the disrespectful kids would not be disciplined. Norma explained that they were re-enrolled in the middle-school class, although they were too old for it. One parent, who occupied a visible position in the church, had already cheerily cornered Lindsay—not to apologize or address her child's problematic behavior—but to explain her child's personality. Lindsay clearly didn't understand her feisty little dear. Lindsay had just listened in disbelief.

As Lindsay trudged to her classroom after hearing Norma's words, the sassiest girls passed her in the hallway and openly mocked her as they strutted past her classroom doorway to join the junior high class. "Lord, give me strength for this week's adventure," she prayed softly, with irony.

Loaded down with "teaching" material and burdened by Norma's words, the attitudes of the kids, and the well-meaning parent, she reached the door to the classroom. Before she could give it a push, the door flung open and a fleeing teen stopped just short of collision with her. The other kids stopped their rough-housing to witness the near-accident. It was as if a foul smell entered the room when she walked in. Total avoidance. No eye contact. Silence.

Lindsay didn't bother to unpack her bags of material. She sat down at the lunchroom table around which their folding chairs were strewn and said, "Let's pray." She reached for hands on either side of her and gripped reluctant fingers. Usually the kids laughed and joked through prayer, mimicked their parents' prayers, or treated it like a comedy routine. Now there was long, unaccustomed silence. The kids fidgeted, a few snatched their hands away, and a few stealthy punches were thrown. Lindsay let the disquieting silence reign. It felt like hours, but Lindsay waited.

In the two weeks prior she had tried to teach them some principles of group prayer: to pray as the Spirit led, not under compulsion or for show; to pray in their natural voices and in everyday words. No one had seemed to hear her.

Finally, Lance said, "Lord, help us have a good class today. Amen."

"Amen," they said in unison, laughing and snickering.

"Thanks for praying, Lance," Lindsay said. "I have something I want us to talk about as a class, so everyone gather together." Sitting at the table with them, Lindsay momentarily had their attention. "I'm new to teaching people your age. I don't know what I'm doing. So I need you to tell me what would make this class worth coming to for you."

"Games," Shanna said.

"Yeah, Bible games," said Jacen.

"Why do you need Sunday school for that?" Lindsay asked.

No one responded.

She waited a few seconds and said, "There are three things every Christian needs to know to live a successful Christian life."

They stared at her. No one asked and no one offered any ideas. Their eyes looked hungry to know. She just looked at them.

"I know one is tithing," said Brad, with an everybody-knows-this-stuff tone.

"Not having sex until you're married," said Tiffany, who had heard it all before.

"The three things necessary for a successful Christian life are praying effectively, being able to fellowship with other Christians, and knowing how to handle the Bible to get answers to life's questions and problems," said Lindsay. "Prayer, fellowship, Bible."

"Yeah, right," said Brad. "We know that. We learned all that last year."

"Uh-huh," said Tiffany and Shanna.

"If you learned all about fellowship, then why didn't you call Jacen by his real name last week?" asked Lindsay, knowing the entire class understood she was referring to when Shanna had called him a "faggot." They had all "oohed" and Jacen had threatened her, saying what he would do if she wasn't a girl and he wasn't in church.

"Nobody's perfect," Shanna retorted.

"Exactly. That's why we need to keep learning about prayer, fellowship, and God's Word the Bible," said Lindsay. "I'm certainly not perfect. I'm asking for your help in making this class good."

"Can we go on trips?" asked Tiffany.

"That's a great way to build your fellowship skills," agreed Lindsay. "Will someone write these on the board?"

Jalil hopped up and grabbed the chalk.

"Okay, what else?" asked Lindsay.

"No memorization," said Shanna.

"We're saying what we *do* want," Lindsay corrected mildly.

"Let's write a magazine," said Lance.

"No, no, no, you always want to write something," screamed Shanna, who is Lance's sister.

"Yeah," said Tiffany, "writing is *school*."

"Then what?" asked Lance. "You all ain't coming up with nothing."

Lindsay silently thanked God for Lance and Jalil, who stood with chalk and eraser in hand, echoing Lance, "C'mon."

There was an awkward silence and when it was apparent no one had anything to suggest, Lindsay said, "Listen, I told you I'm new at teaching senior high, but I've been teaching the Bible for twenty years. May I make a suggestion and we can see if it works? If it doesn't work, we can drop it and try something else."

"Okay."

"Okay."

"Okay."

She looked from face to face and when everyone had nodded or affirmed, she said. "Let's plan three outings where we can fellowship—"

"Cool."

"True dat." Their interrupting chorus was totally positive and unified.

"Let's commit ourselves to sharing and group prayer for the first twenty minutes of class. And let's read the book of Mark together."

"The whole book?! We can't read the whole book!"

"Pray for twenty minutes? I mean, what's to say for twenty whole minutes?"

"We'll fall asleep."

"This is crazy."

"Yeah."

"Have any one of you ever read a whole book of the Bible?" asked Lindsay.

Silence.

"Of course not," Shanna said.

"Why do you say it like that?" asked Lindsay.

"Because those books are long," replied Tiffany.

"Who has their Bible?" asked Lindsay. "No one. Okay, Jalil, would you go to the sanctuary and ask an usher to let you bring back ten Bibles, please?"

As they thumbed through the Bible to find Mark, Shanna, who found it first, said, "See, look how long it is."

"How many chapters?"

"Uh, sixteen," said Lance.

"So, if we read a chapter a week we could finish in four months easily."

"A chapter a week!" exclaimed Tiffany.

"How long is the longest chapter? How many verses?"

"Whoa, wait, I got it—chapter fourteen," said Brad, as they all flipped the pages. "D—. Sorry. Seventy-two verses. Seventy-two verses in one chapter. That's a lot."

"That *is* a lot, but that's the longest chapter. If you read some each day, how many verses would you have to read a day?"

"Ten."

"Yeah, ten."

"Ten."

Their voices sounded like bells ringing, and their faces were like lanterns being lit by a flame.

"What do you think? Could you read—at the most because this is the longest chapter—ten verses a day?"

"Two days you'd have to read eleven verses," harped Shanna.

"Or you could read twelve verses one day," suggested Tiffany.

"What do you think? Could you do it?"

Most agreed but a few waffled.

"Well, when will you do your reading? I know you have tons of homework and chores and stuff your parents want you to do, and you'll have to really make time, right?" asked Lindsay.

"Got that. My schedule is jammed," said Lance. "I'll have to do mine on the train. I see people reading the Bible on the subway all the time."

"I'm gonna do mine sixth period," said Tiffany. Shanna nodded in agreement.

"Can everybody see some time you can squeeze it in?" asked Lindsay gently.

"Mm-mm" was the uniform reply.

"So do we have to do something else beside read? I mean is there gonna be like a quiz or something?" asked Shanna.

"No. We'll read it during the week and then we'll discuss what we've read in class."

"Discuss it?" asked Lance.

"Yeah," said Lindsay. "We'll talk about what you thought about what you read. Do you like it, not like it, agree with it, disagree with it, understand it, relate to it, whatever."

"Disagree with the Bible! You can have an opinion on the Bible?!" exclaimed Tiffany. All eyes were on Lindsay, questioning, waiting for the blasphemy.

"Mm-hmm. I can't wait to hear what some of you will have to say about what you read in Mark."

"Got dat!"

There was general high-fiving and descent into play before they held hands to pray. Lance again led, but this time several others said brief prayers. Lindsay wanted to cry—but this time tears of joy—when Jalil prayed, "Lord, thank you for a new class."

Only one of the expelled students returned; the prima donnas remained in the middle-school class. In the weeks and months following, Lindsay learned, to her surprise, that the kids who remained all came to Sunday school voluntarily. She also learned that of the seven boys, only two lived in a home with a father. She discovered that the kids were not brats. Rather, as she began reading the gospel of Mark with them, she began to feel the weight of their adolescent challenges, especially the five fatherless boys.

Lindsay's prayer list expanded to include ten teenagers and their parents and guardians, with man-sized prayers for five of the boys. Her life was already more than full when she received her Sunday school assignment. Now with an ever-challenging class and their trips, there was no time, it seemed, to pray for these new young men in her life.

But prayer was her only option as she perceived their needs more and more. So many of the basic applications of the faith were missing in the lives of these boys, who were very soon to be men. They had no daily examples of life lived as a Christian man. Their thinking and emotions were almost wholly shaped by the media, encounters on the street, social interaction at school, and misinformation from other teens.

Two months after she began teaching the class, one of her favorites, fourteen-year-old Jordan, was arrested for fighting at school. She prayed fervently to no avail for his release during the three months he awaited trial. His sentence was a harsh nine to twelve months in juvenile detention—jail. Lindsay accompanied Jordan's mother to his court dates and meetings with their attorney. It was all Lindsay could do to hold back tears when Jordan was brought into the courtroom in shackles.

But Lindsay didn't cry when she heard Jordan's sentence. The months of teaching senior high Sunday school had toughened her up. It also firmed her resolve that God had a plan for these young lives.

Convinced that Jordan's mom was doing as much as a mother could do, she felt that Jordan, and all the boys in her class, needed men in their lives. Certainly there was no magic road that one came through adolescence unscathed if one had a father, but she noted without exception that the boys who had strong Christian dads had better means of coping with their teen challenges. They weren't necessarily "better" kids in terms of behavior or faith, but they certainly had someone helping them navigate these tough years and that made their lives smoother.

Lindsay began to pray for each of the boys in her class. She prayed for them by name in her quiet time and found herself often absorbed by thoughts of "her kids." She remembered the funny things they said in class: "Do you know what a whoremonger is?" she'd asked. "A playa," Brad had responded without skipping a beat as he read. She relived her joy at watching them learn to puzzle through the meaning of parables. She reflected on what she had learned from them. For example, they compared the Sadducees to the death-with-no-afterlife philosophy of some hip-hop icons. She caught glimpses of the men God wanted to emerge from their lanky or still baby-fat frames and determined to set up one-on-one Bible studies to disciple each one into a godly manhood.

"We tried to do that and it never worked," Norma replied when Lindsay suggested the idea. "The men who could do it don't have time. They're serving in important roles in the church."

"Is it okay if I ask around?" asked Lindsay.

"Sure."

As a rather plain, fifty-something divorced woman with no children, Lindsay was the least likely person to rally men in the church around the needs of teenage boys, but finding Bible-study mentors was at the top of her prayer list and in her thoughts whenever an idle moment arose. The very next Sunday, one of the elders approached her about Bible-study mentoring one of the most challenging, disruptive male students in her class—his grandson.

"We've been praying for a way to handle him," said the elder, "Your idea is a godsend."

Lindsay prayed prayers of joy and continued to ask God for mentors. She knew few men in the church and had no idea who to ask or how to search. She just prayed that God would provide the boys with mentors.

Without an announcement or notice in the church program or on a bulletin board, word spread in the church. In lots of unusual ways, but with amazing speed, mentors—every one a strong, committed, mature Christian man—stepped forward. Every man said he had been previously feeling the call on his life to mentor boys in the church. Lindsay watched God match fatherless boys in her class with male mentors, including Jordan, whose mentor wrote and called him while he was in jail. She also witnessed the fathers who *were* in the home begin one-on-one Bible studies with their sons.

As they read Mark 6 about the disciples witnessing miracles, Lindsay mused that she was witnessing miracles. The class was still constantly challenging, but now the atmosphere was usually joyfully frenetic. The kids came willingly. The mentored boys visibly lived out their faith more.

Lindsay continues to pray and give thanks. She still weeps sometimes. For example, she couldn't hold back tears when one formerly drug-addicted dad joined his son's study, saying almost shyly, "I think this is what I'm supposed to do as a father."

——————

All of us have at some point felt like Lindsay, that the needs of someone we were praying for were so big that we could spend forty hours a week on our knees and it still wouldn't be enough time to express them all to God and hear a word from

God on each. We have all felt too small, inadequate against the needs. And we all have limits on the time we can devote to prayer. But take heart, God has no limitations, and God has given us a simple way to pray effectively for the men we care about so deeply.

1 Thessalonians 5:16–18 encourages us to "Be joyful always; pray continually ("without ceasing" KJV); give thanks in all circumstances . . ."

These three guidelines provide a basis for developing a prayer life for man-sized concerns when we don't have a lot of time to pray.

1. Note something to be happy about regarding the man in your prayers.
2. Live a life of prayer: pray *through* situations, not just in crises.
3. Thank God for all circumstances, enjoyable or not. Even when you don't understand why things are occurring, know God is working on the man (and you!).

Prayer 14
Lord, teach me to pray.

He Brings Me Joy

The words "you bring me joy" from an enduring pop song by Anita Baker sum up how we need to apply 1 Thessalonians 5:16 to the men in our lives. Start now by writing down a list of things you are happy about regarding the man for whom

you are praying. Be sure to invite the Holy Spirit
into this process. If you can't make a list that numbers at least a half dozen, keep working at it until
you do. Pray this:

Prayer 15
You've told me to be joyful about _____
_____, and I know there are things about him that
bring joy to your heart, Lord. Show me those
facets of him via your Holy Spirit, and let me have
the joy of appreciating those qualities in him.

This list of six "joys" will be the basis for your
first week of prayer. Post it where you can refer to
it often and add to it as the Spirit reveals other
aspects of this man's character, personality, gifts,
deeds, words, thoughts, feelings, and other attrib-
utes that bring you joy.

Remember Lindsay's example. She replayed in
her mind the funny, clever, incisive things the kids
said and did. Zechariah 4:10 urges us not to despise
small things. Don't overlook them in the men in
your prayer life.

Praying in Snatches

1 Thessalonians 5:17 encourages us to pray continually. It's popular in our busy world today to
advise everyone to set aside a specific period of
prayer time or quiet time each day. I encourage those
of you who have incorporated this discipline of
prayer into your daily life. Regular prayer is crucial

to Christian growth, but you do not need to have a routine to pray effectively for the men in your life. And for those who have set aside times for prayer and devotion, those times may not be enough for all the man-sized needs.

You don't have to overhaul your schedule to find an extra hour or even fifteen minutes of retreat in order to bring the needs of the men you love before God. I know many women who feel disappointed in themselves and frustrated when they can't find time to be alone with God or when they sacrifice that time for some pressing concern or even a much needed nap. The emphasis on the need for prayer has somehow been misunderstood as the need for a rigid, inflexible prayer routine. That makes prayer another item on the busy woman's to-do list, another activity that is hard to find time to perform. Prayer is not meant to be hard. God is not on the same list of demands on your time with your husband, kids, mother, siblings, friends, boss, coworkers, congregants, club members, and on and on.

As Christians, we are able to access God anywhere, anytime. (But not anyhow. We must approach God through Jesus Christ.) In Christ, we always, everywhere have access to God. With such total access, we don't need a rigid schedule or routine to pray effectively. Praying continually frees us to offer up prayers to God at anytime. We don't need a formal routine, a specific time and place, or a preset format. We need only learn to pray in snatches.

We snatch moments and pray, just as we might take a moment for a quick refreshing drink or tasty morsel to nourish us during a busy day. I've learned to pray in traffic jams, even while parking!

In the classic book *Prayer: Conversing with God,* Rosalind Rinker names the four elements that make snatch prayers effective: natural, short, silence, listening. The purpose is to express our hearts to God and allow God to commune with us.

The more *natural* our prayer, the more real God becomes. As you grab a moment to pray for the men in your life, ask yourself: Do I speak this way to anyone else? Am I talking with God as the real "me"? Lindsay's ironic prayer, "Lord, give me strength for this week's adventure," was natural. If we approach the Lord with reverence, God can handle irony, anger, the entire range of our feelings. Effective prayer means being real with God.

The goal is to remove the traditionalism and "put on" habits that keep us from being real with God. Replace "thee, thou, thy, thine" with "you, your, yours." Talk as you do in everyday speech. God understands bad grammar, street lingo, anything that is spoken from the heart. Do not put on "proper" speech, if that is not how you normally talk. React naturally to the feelings your prayers ignite in you—nervousness, joy, sorrow, anger, fear—knowing God accepts your full range of emotions and requires only *honesty,* but avoid working yourself up into unnatural overemotion. The same rules of self-control that apply to ordinary conversation apply to conversational prayer. When praying, don't raise your voice or shout unnaturally. Simply speak with God as someone present with you, and know that God is present and doesn't need to be named every few words. "I'm here, God, in your presence, Lord, and just calling on your name, dear Lord, and I just want you, oh Lord, to know, dear God, that, oh Lord . . ." Imagine someone spoke to you like that: "I'm here, Karen, in your presence, Karen, and just calling on your name, dear Karen . . ." The natural thing to say would be, "Karen, I'm glad you're here . . ." Likewise, in prayer it's more natural to say, "Lord, I'm glad you are here with me, and I pray in the power of your name."

Pray about one thing, in a *short* utterance. ("Lord, thank you for _____'s new job and his hardworking nature.") Check yourself if you have prayed more than a sentence or two or if you have prayed about more than a single subject. (Not, "Lord, thank you for _____'s new job and help him to magnify you as he works as supervisor, and bless my family and help us to find the new house we want now that we have more money, and help us to tithe, and bless my brother Ralph with a new job too and his family, and I lift up Robin's cousin who was in the car accident, and...") Lindsay's prayers were short. God heard and answered.

Embrace *silences,* knowing that God needs time to speak. Private prayer is a dialogue, not a monologue. God speaks in the silences. "Be still, and know that I am God," Psalm 46:10 says. We learn of God in the silences. As Lindsay allowed the silences during group prayer with the teenagers, she allowed God to speak to them and to her.

Listen to God in the silences. Listen for the thoughts God's Spirit places in your mind after you have prayed. Often these thoughts will feel totally foreign to you. That's because God's thoughts are not our thoughts (Isaiah 55:8). The easiest way to recognize these "thought responses" of God is to test them against God's principles. If the thought is judgmental, vindictive, self-pitying, it is likely your own. If it is loving, joyful, peaceful, patient, kind, good, faithful, gentle, or self-controlling, it is likely from God (Galatians 5:22–23).

Had Lindsay's thoughts been to punish or retaliate against the teens when she prayed with them, those would clearly have been her thoughts. Hearing their needs and ministering the Word of God to them, were clearly pricked by God's Spirit.

Listen also for Scriptures the Spirit of God brings to your memory or that come up in conversation with others after you have prayed. Such Scriptures may be God talking with you and providing text for you to use in praying for the men in your life. As we discussed in the previous chapter, listening is a critical skill. It's even more important in communicating with God. As we snatch moments to pray, God later snatches our attention back—if we are sensitive—at various times in answer to our prayer.

Be sure to place yourself in an environment to hear God. Get away from busyness and get down to "God's business." Lindsay might have kept her class busy with the show-and-tell, Christian pop music, and other paraphernalia, but may never have reached their hearts without prayer and those awkward silences during which God—not Lindsay—related to the teens.

Thanks in All Things

This way of praying for men may be different from your usual prayers, but if you are reading this book, you likely want different answers than you have been receiving, or perhaps you haven't received any answers and want to hear from God. There's an old saying: Do what you've always done and you'll get what you've always gotten. Start finding new words to articulate your thoughts and feelings to God and new ways to listen to God.

With your list of joys, start finding snatches of time to give *thanks* to God for the man you're praying for, rather than making appeal after appeal. Lindsay recalled the funny things the teens said in class, their quickness in interpreting Scripture, and the things she learned from *them*. She reflected on her joys in them, not just on their needs and how they challenged her.

In brief, natural prayers, give thanks to God as often during the day as the subject of your prayers pops into your thoughts. Ask God to speak back to you, to respond to your prayers of joy.

When we cannot make time to pray, remember we can communicate with God in the time we *have* by making snatch prayers a part of everything we do.

Prayer 16
Thank you, Lord Jesus, for [one of your joys in the man for whom you are praying]. Thank you for revealing this part of his nature to me. You created him, and I'm glad to know him and to share in his good qualities.

And then, as you pray continually, listen continually.

Learn

Even they who were scornful on that day of small beginnings shall rejoice.

Zechariah 4:10 NAB

Unlearn

List some of the "unanswered" prayers regarding the man you are bringing before God. Next to each "unanswered" prayer, list something about that man that brings you joy.

Prayer 17

[Be in silence with God for whatever time your schedule permits.]

7

Praying that God's Will, Not Ours, Be Done

God wants what's best

God never calls us in the New Testament to "seek His will," but rather to seek His kingdom and do His will.... Rather than talk about "seeking the will of God," we ought to speak of following the guidance of God.

If you are struggling with a specific question, rather than trying to magically divine God's answer, spend time drawing close to Him.

Bruce Waltke, *Knowing the Will of God*

When God answered no to a woman's prayer for her husband, it led her to discover that God's will was larger and better than she ever envisioned.

Otto's lung was inoperable, the doctors said, and they informed him that his life was coming to an end. It was hard for Edith to believe Otto was ill. He had not changed at all. His voice had always been rather high pitched and breathy, so there was no indication in his speech that his lungs were diseased. His manner of speaking and his wiry frame had, in fact, hidden his power all his life. He was still the tall, skinny, soft-spoken man of God who had earned the respect of everyone who knew him.

Even his appearance hadn't changed perceptibly in thirty years. He'd been called "Elder Holmes" for forty years because of his spiritual maturity, his iron-willed walk with God since his youth, not because of his numerical age—eighty years.

Three times God honored Edith's fervent prayer requests and kept the hand of death from her husband of forty-five years. After a similar pronouncement from the doctors nearly a decade before, Otto and Edith's children had given them a gift to travel to the Holy Land. To everyone's surprise, Otto had hiked the rugged terrain to sites of Christian history he had so avidly read about and participated fully in the activities of the tour. Once they returned home, Otto began cutting back on his activities, heeding the doctor's prediction of his eminent death. But that didn't last long. He was known as a wise, sensitive, nonjudgmental elder who always seemed to offer the right balance of sage counsel and firm correction. His no-appointment-needed, open-door policy resulted ironically in an office whose door was almost always closed, as parishioner after parishioner shared confidences with Elder Otto. Soon, by sheer response to demand, he was again keeping more than full-time hours at his tiny hovel in the church building.

During a decade of active life, the doctors' prognoses became a dim memory, forgotten except during prayer when Otto and Edith, their family, or their church routinely asked God to heal him and extend his years. Now with this new diagnosis from the best veteran's hospital in the region, Edith immediately set herself to the task of prayer.

Fifteen years younger than Otto, Edith had just retired from a career begun late in her life, after their four children were nearly grown. She was looking forward to the first time in their long, happy marriage, which had been filled with rearing children and ministering to others, when they would both be free to enjoy time together. She prayed as she had prayed for more than a decade— for God's healing and for God to extend Otto's years. But Otto asked her to change her prayers.

"For years we've been asking God to heal me and give me more years," he said to her gently, as they drove up the driveway to their favorite bed-and-breakfast. They had decided to make a weekend getaway shortly after the pronouncement from the doctors. "I'm not being led to pray that anymore," he continued, in a matter-of-fact tone.

Edith said nothing. She wondered if Otto was giving up on life, and then slowly asked, "Is your back hurting you?" How a visit to the doctor for a backache had turned into a diagnosis of inoperable lung cancer was still a medical mystery to her.

"No, sugar," he said, harking back to their dating days, when she had been a nineteen-year-old, fresh from the South, having come North in search of a job to earn money to return to college. He had been a much-sought-after bachelor deacon in his thirties. He had called her "sugar" as many of the older Southern-born men addressed women who could be their daughters, but they had both known right away that he spoke to her man to woman. "I feel good," he continued. "That painkiller they gave me for my back is working."

She looked toward him and felt like the same highly favored princess of God she had been when she first struck his fancy. He still made her heart skip. She was still instinctively coy with him: She *didn't* ask him if he meant he was ready to die.

"I'm not saying I'm ready to die, honey. I'm not saying that at all. I love being here with y'all. I'm prepared, with God's help, to fight this growth."

"Whew." She was surprised by her own audible sigh. He could still read her inexpressible emotions and converse with her soul, as he had from their first times together nearly a half century ago.

Otto turned off the engine. The car sat parked in front of the picturesque bed-and-breakfast. He leaned across the gear shift, stretching his seat belt to the maximum, and nosed her ear. "I'm saying, Edible Edith . . ."

She giggled spontaneously, and leaned her head in his direction. She was always grateful to God that her "driver's side" ear retained its hearing. The hearing aid was needed only in her right ear.

". . . that I want my life to glorify God. I don't want to die, but I'm ready. If more years will give God glory, amen. If my dying will give God glory, amen." He nudged her face and kissed away the first tear that dotted her cheek, and then the next one, and when the tears were a stream, he made the back of his bony hand a sponge and simply pressed it gently against her cheek, first on one side and then the other.

He climbed the stairs to their favorite room overlooking the lake much more slowly than in times remembered. He held the rail with one hand and their overnight bag, which he insisted on carrying, with the other. He paused on the landing to take her hand and help her up the last few steps, as he had since their honeymoon.

In the beautifully adorned room, they didn't dash for the king-sized four poster bed and dive under its lacy covers as they had done when their four privacy-snatchers lived at home and they had conquered the monumental tasks of planning a weekend getaway. Instead, Otto reached for Edith's hand and led her to the two easy chairs by the window and said, "Let's pray."

"Lord, show me what to pray," Edith moaned.

"Dear sovereign, majestic, all-loving God," began Otto. "You are the God we have so often loved to call our Jehovah Raffah, God our healer. And, Lord, thank you for being my healer. Thank you for these ten years of my life where you have confounded even the wise, just as your Word says. You have shown yourself more knowing than these good doctors. I am grateful to you, Lord. I am."

"Thank you, Lord," Edith mouthed, through sobs.

"Now Lord, we have this new word from the doctors. But you knew about this cancer since before the beginning of time. You know all about my body. You know all about the growth. And more important, you know all about my orders here on earth. You know what your purpose was for me when you gave me life. Lord, you know where I've made your heart glad in fulfilling my orders, and you know where I've disappointed you, where I've come up short, knowingly or unknowingly. I know you've forgiven me where I've fallen short.

"Lord Jesus," he continued, "I'm not asking for more time than whatever is in your divine plan. I'm asking that I bring you glory. If being a husband, a father, a grandfather, an elder among your people, if that brings you the most glory, then I pray that you enable me in every way—in my spirit, in my emotions, in my mind and, yes Lord, in my body— to fulfill those responsibilities. But, if leaving this body and coming to be with you brings you the most glory, then help me to lay this body down like I hang up my favorite overcoat when spring comes. Whichever seems right to you, Lord."

Otto's pause and then the long silence were Edith's opportunity to voice her prayers. But she could not. Her heart was breaking. She did not want whatever seemed right to God. She wanted her husband to be healthy and live. She wanted to celebrate their golden anniversary, at the very least. That wasn't too much to ask God. There wasn't a single cell in her body, a single tremor of her emotions, a single thread of her thoughts that wanted whatever God might decide. She wanted God to decide in her favor.

Edith knew Otto needed her prayers. He needed her to "touch and agree" (Matthew 18:19 KJV) with him in prayer. She also knew God well enough to require herself to be honest in her prayers. So she refused to pray.

"Amen," she said after the silence continued an interminable amount of time.

Otto did not let go of her hand. She stared out on the lake and then at Otto, whose eyes remained closed, his chin tilted slightly upward.

"Lord," he began slowly, "please show the glory of your will to my wife. Show her, Lord, so she can love your will with the same passionate, steadfast, active love that she has loved me with. Show her the glory of your will, Lord, so she can demonstrate her love for your will the same way she has so powerfully demonstrated her love for me. I'm grateful to you, Lord, for that June Sunday I first saw her gorgeous legs in Little Light Gospel Church choir practice. Thank you, Lord, that I have known the greatest love that life on earth can offer. Reward this good woman, Lord; reward her with the confidence in your will that is greater than anything else in this world."

She gripped Otto's hand and through shaking sobs, cried out, "Lord, not my will but thy will be done! Help me to mean it; help me to mean it."

When they returned to church the following Sunday, their pastor announced Otto's illness and asked the church to join him in prayer for his healing. After the prayer, Otto rose from his pew and walked toward the pulpit. The pastor, a man half Otto's age whom Otto had been instrumental in calling to the church, watched with a puzzled look as Otto, uninvited, climbed the few stairs. When Otto reached him, the pastor stepped aside to let him speak: "I'm grateful for your prayers, saints. Those of today and over all these years." The church was hushed, and only the sound of his soft, serious voice could be heard. "But I want you to pray this for me—not that I be healed but that *God's will* be done and that I bring glory to God." There were many misty eyes, and after the service Edith was deluged with questions about Otto's life expectancy. Was it weeks, months? What could they do?

A year passed. It was a sweet time. Otto's illness progressed in a way that was only noticeable in a slight reduction of his busy schedule and a sense that he moved more slowly and began, for the first time in his four score years, to be an elderly man. He looked the same and seemed more spiritually powerful than ever. He was still growing in the Lord and remained a major asset to the ministry of their church. His personal ministry to his neighbors, family, and associates continued unabated. Edith, always the favored child of God, believed God had again given her the desire of her heart. And as the months turned into a year, the dire diagnosis, just like the others, lost its urgency.

Then one afternoon Otto had to be taken to the emergency room. He was released after a few days but declined rapidly in the following week. He was tired and weak. Those were the only visible indications of the state of his health, so he and Edith decided he could receive those who asked to visit. They came literally in hundreds. A party atmosphere lingered in their home, day after day, as friends and family came to show their love to Otto, bringing food, gifts, old photos, and laughter. Old friendships were renewed and many of Otto's non-Christian acquaintances were welcomed into the community of believers.

Otto grew wearier and wearier and finally asked to be taken to the hospital. There he called his four children to him and laid his hands on each of them in private, blessing them and also charging them with specifics for their future. He gave Edith instructions, revealing the hiding places of small stashes of cash and reminding her of the order of their financial affairs. Alone with her in the sunny hospital room, he held her hand with his free hand, for the other one was hooked to an IV tube. Her tears dripped onto the white sheets. She knew if he had the strength, he would kiss them away. The joy of a shared lifetime was expressed in their silence.

"Ask Carlene to come in and bathe me," he said, referring to his nephew Ed's wife, a registered nurse. He had raised his nephew almost as a son and Carlene was like a daughter-in-law. Edith wanted to be with him when he died and did not want to leave his bedside. "Go and get her," he said, gently nudging Edith's hand. "I want my body to be clean when I leave."

When she was finished, Carlene entered the waiting room. The family searched her eyes for the verdict, but she simply told them they could go back into his room. Edith, their four children, spouses, several of their eight grandchildren, Ed, and Carlene gathered around Otto's bed. Edith was gripping his hand as he breathed his last breath. The sun lingered on his face. Despite the whimpering and sobs, a silence seemed to hover over the room, like a blanket of peace. They would later share with each other their experiences at the moment of Otto's death and describe their sorrow as that wonderful tired feeling after a monumental accomplishment. Each used almost the same words to describe the aura in the room at Otto's passing— sweet sadness.

Edith mourned. A gregarious woman, with a voice as booming as Otto's was soft, she wept and cried and prayed aloud. The children and his pastor planned the funeral, and she felt as if she were sleepwalking through those initial days after Otto died. She was sitting in the front pew at the funeral service when Otto's words at the bed-and-breakfast came back to her. She suddenly understood. It was as if she was being awakened from slumber. "If leaving this body and coming to be with you brings you the most glory, then help me to lay this body down like I hang up my favorite overcoat when spring comes. Whichever seems right to you, Lord."

Edith looked around the church, which held more than seven hundred comfortably, and marveled at the standing-room-only crowd. Otto had not been a celebrity. He had worked as a bus driver and then retired on a modest pension. He had not been a war hero. He had served his country as an enlisted man in the segregated armed forces and quietly returned to civilian life where he was often treated as a second-class citizen. Later Edith would be told that passers-by had asked whose funeral it was, judging by the crowds that the funeral was for a VIP.

The service opened with a rendition of Otto's favorite hymn; it seemed to shake the rafters of the 150-year-old edifice and then continued in a series of simple, brief testimonials, so numerous that they ran over three hours. No one left the service, and the hours felt like minutes as stories came forth of lives touched and transformed by this thin man with a high-pitched voice. His sons, daughter, their spouses, and his grandchildren were a living testimony to him, and when they spoke about the man up close and private, his awesome inner depths were revealed.

Edith was rapt, listening to the scores of testimonies of those who had come from near and far to acknowledge her husband's important role in their lives. They were old and young; black, white, and Asian; rich and struggling through poverty; well-educated and plain spoken; and in such a wide sphere of professions that, although she had experienced it day-by-day, she could still barely conceive how Otto had encountered all these people. Every single testimony related Scripture or scriptural guidance Otto had provided.

She had attended camp meetings, huge public outreaches, stadium rallies by major evangelists, and megachurch services, yet nothing equaled the spiritual fervor, the witness for the living God that surrounded Edith at Otto's funeral service. She was speechless. "This is what you meant," she said out loud to him, amidst a din of cheers of praise to God as another story of homage to the testator ended. "You knew even your death could give God glory, big-time glory," she whispered to Otto, using a phrase they often borrowed from their youngest grandchild.

His casket was closed. Very late into the night, when all the testimonials that could be heard had been given, the cover was lifted. The procession for last respects took more than an hour, and finally when Edith looked at Otto's peaceful face for the last time, she understood Otto's prayer that God's will be done.

She understood it better in the months and years that followed, for she heard story after story of how deeply Otto's funeral and the words spoken there had affected so many. Some who had turned away from God returned to the faith. Backsliders regained their forward momentum. Doubters strengthened their resolve. Many who had become tired were encouraged to stick with God to the end of their own lives. Otto had given a profound witness for Jesus Christ even in his death, and his witness continued to live.

Over the months in her solitary moments, Edith relived her special times with Otto. She remembered his prayer in the bed-and-breakfast: "Reward this good woman, Lord; reward her with the confidence in your will that is greater than anything else in this world." And she discovered that God had answered his prayer. God had replaced her reliance on Otto with an even greater trust in God's will, and each day she grew more and more excited about discovering what God's will was for her in this new season of her life.

God knows everything. Your best understanding of the man or men you pray for is minuscule in comparison with God's. Your sharpest listening skills and most spiritual discernment cannot provide you the same understanding as God's. Our thoughts are not God's thoughts (Isaiah 55:8).

So, as you pray, your requests need to be God's intentions. God's intentions are the best possible. This means learning to seek God's guidance, to listen to God, and to recognize God's "voice" when God's intent is revealed to you as distinct from your own desires.

The key is to ask what God's will is and to pray for that instead of what you want for the men in your life. Your prayer for the man you're interceding for might be that he be saved, or get a better job, or stop watching so much TV, or spend time with you and the kids. Those prayers are likely for you and may have little to do with God's will.

Even if you feel you already know what to pray for, start with this simple prayer.

Prayer 18
Sovereign Lord, you know _____ far better than I do. Thank you for his _____ and other things you have shown me about him that bring me joy. You created him. You sustain his life. You have a wonderful purpose for him. Show me what you

> specifically want me to pray for regarding
> _____ . Allow me to help accom-
> plish *your* will in him through this prayer.

Once you have asked God to show you what to
pray, you have aligned your will with God's purpose. Let go of your old prayers, the ones in which
you thought or felt you knew best. Do not say
those prayers anymore. Prayer is conversing with
God, so if you find yourself resorting to those old
prayers, interrupt yourself and replace your words
with a prayer seeking God's will. For example,

"Lord, please help him quit—no Lord, show *me*
what you specifically want me to pray for regarding
_____. I want what you want for him.
I trust you know best."

Four Ways to God's Will

Look for the prayers God wants you to pray in
four ways: by reading the Bible, in words spoken
by mature Christians (pastor or spiritual leader),
in circumstances, and in your silent times of Christian meditation.

1. Bible Reading

The example of Otto and Edith illustrates how
Otto drew from God's Word to discover God's
will. Nothing can replace a regular reading of the
Bible so God can speak to you from your knowledge of Scripture.

Suppose you want the man you are interceding for to come to know God. Your Bible reading during this time might have led you to 2 Peter 3:8–9:

> But do not forget this one thing, dear friends: With the Lord a day is like a thousand years, and a thousand years are like a day. The Lord is not slow in keeping his promise, as some understand slowness. He is patient with you, not wanting anyone to perish, but everyone to come to repentance.

God wants everyone to be saved, so your will and God's will are in harmony. But examine the Scripture fully before you pray and note the emphasis on time and patience. Rather than praying simply for salvation ("Lord, please bring _____ into a relationship with you …"), God may be leading you to pray specifically for time and patience ("Sovereign Lord, thank you for _____'s good qualities such as _____ that make me glad he is in my life. Please bear with him while he is searching and let him discover his own need for a turnaround.").

God's will might be that you exhibit patience with him and yourself.

2. Conversation with Mature Christians

Edith learned from her relationship with Otto, a mature Christian, God's will in their encounter with death. Our relationships with other Christians who have a strong walk with the Lord are invaluable for knowing God's will. God will speak to us through them.

3. Observe Unfolding Circumstances

What Yogi Berra said, "You can observe a whole lot by looking," applies to discerning God's will. Watch what unfolds in the circumstances. The circumstances of Otto's illness revealed God's will—slowly at first, but then more noticeably.

4. Silence Before God

The silent times in Otto and Edith's prayers allowed them to open themselves to discerning God's will. Silence in our prayers, as mentioned in the previous chapter, are key in discerning God's will for us.

Whose Will Is It Anyway—Mine or God's?

Sometimes we struggle to distinguish God's will from our own. Acknowledge what your will is, just as Edith did. Ask God, as did Edith, to help you accept whatever God's will is. Then relax and continue to pray with confidence that God's plan—or at least, the piece of the plan that you need to know—will be revealed to you.

Discovering God's will is a constant process of testing and adjustment. Surprisingly, for most of us, the hardest part is not "hearing" from God, but getting ourselves out of the way. God's intent is expressed in that proverbial still small voice, while our own opinions, judgments, and desires are like clanging gongs and cymbals.

Even during quiet times of Bible reading, meditation, and prayer, our own thoughts—not God's—may be our central focus for a long time before we learn to properly distinguish the whisper of God from our own inner noise. It can be frustrating to want to hear from God, and yet not be sure that what you think you heard was from God. Do not agonize about this.

Imagine you start a new job in a department with lots of other employees. Each one is busy talking on the telephone and all of them pause to call out to you for one thing or another throughout the day. At first, you do not distinguish the boss's voice from the others, and therefore might not give the boss's request the expected high priority. Soon, however, you learn to distinguish the boss's voice amidst all the others and drop what you are doing and respond right away when the boss calls.

Have you ever been to a swimming pool where dozens of toddlers are in the water making a loud cacophony of squeals, laughter, and shrieks while a group of mothers congregate on the edge, a stone's throw away, totally absorbed in their own conversation? At the cry of "Mommy!" all the mothers' heads will turn, but one mother will rise in a split instant. She knows her child's voice, amidst all the children's voices.

I remember calling home from Africa and having a terrible connection, yet my mother instantly knew my voice. I was her child and we had a stronger connection than mere technology could impede.

So it is with knowing God's voice. As you pray constantly—talking with God regularly and frequently in snatch prayers and looking for God to talk to you in passages from the Bible and in words spoken by mature Christians—and as you discern God in circumstances and in your silent times of prayer, you will learn to recognize God's communication with you.

Test and See

In the meantime, however, you may be like that employee during the first week on the job or a mother in the maternity ward struggling to distinguish her baby's cry above the din of wails in the hospital nursery. Until you are comfortable discerning God's communication with you, here is a simple check you can use to be more confident you are praying God's will, not yours.

> Do not conform any longer to the pattern of this world, but be transformed by the renewing of your mind. Then you will be able to test and

approve what God's will is—his good, pleasing and perfect will.

Romans 12:2

The test is first on us. We check ourselves to see if we are living by God's standards rather than the social standards around us. The previous verse is a yardstick for doing this self-check.

> **Prayer 19**
> Lord, I admit that I am not living in a way that pleases you regarding [name your problem area]. I realize this sin problem is making it impossible for us to communicate clearly. I know you hear my prayer, but I can't hear you, God. Please help me offer my body as a living sacrifice, holy and pleasing to you as my act of worship that will open up our lines of communication.

Allow God to correct you and make whatever adjustments you need to make in your life to get right with God. God has mercy on everyone, but God honors the prayers of those who live right. Living right means living by God's principles in the Bible. In my experience as a sister-pastor to many, many women, I have observed that moral and attitudinal sins are the biggest reason Christian women experience frustration when they pray for men.

To check that we are praying God's will, not ours, is the second guideline in Romans 12:2, "be transformed by the renewing of your mind." Is your thinking new regarding the man for whom you are interceding? Or are you thinking the same old thoughts you've always had about him? If your list of joyful things about him from chapter 6 is regularly expanding, if you read Scriptures about godly character and think, "Yes, he's a bit like that," if you are discovering valuable things about him that you once took for granted, then your mind is being renewed. Now, you need only allow those new thoughts to transform your prayers and your actions.

When you can honestly examine your words and behavior regarding the man on whose behalf you are interceding and say to God that your attitudes and actions toward him are changed, you can begin to trust that what you *think* is God's intention for him is accurate.

Prayer 20

Lord, thank you for _____'s fine qualities such as _____ that make me know I need to keep speaking to him with real respect [or add other quality of godly speech] and acting _____ [add other quality of godly behavior] toward him. I am humbled by how you are changing my attitude and behavior, and I know this is opening me up to hear with clarity your intentions for him so I can pray in harmony with your will.

These words from the following verse, Romans 12:3, are a yardstick for doing this second self-check: "Do not think of yourself more highly than you ought, but rather think of yourself with sober judgment..."

Until you have humbly tested yourself, you are in danger of mistaking every thought that comes to your mind as the prayer God wants you to make for the man for whom you are interceding. Every prayer will seem good, pleasing, and perfectly God's will, when in fact they are only good to you, pleasing to you, and what you want. If you have tested *you*, Romans 12:2 says you are *then* able to test what God's will is for the man for whom you are praying.

But Nothing's Wrong with My Will...

The tests for God's will are so simple—good, pleasing, perfect—yet can be deceptive if we miss the element of perspective. What is good from God's perspective? What pleases God? What would be perfectly godlike?

There was nothing wrong or ungodly about her will, but Edith's perspective on Otto's illness and God's perspective were very different.

Let's revisit the example above of your first day on a new job. Wouldn't it be great if your new boss took the entire day to sit with you, explain all the aspects of the work as you encounter each new element, introduce you to everyone, remind you of their names as you inevitably forget them, help you find everything you need, and make sure you never feel alone, too challenged, or confused?

The boss has a lot of other staff to supervise and goals that have little or nothing to do with you. The boss must focus on the big goals of the department, of which you are only a small part. The boss's perspective and your perspective are different. The boss's view of the situation is the one that rules the workplace, and if you do your job with an understanding of your boss's perspective—waiting your turn to see or talk with the boss, putting the boss's priorities ahead of your own, relating to colleagues in a way that the boss approves—you will succeed in that department.

Similarly, God loves you and the man for whom you are praying. But God has a purpose for the entire universe, a purpose for which you play an important bit part. Once you understand what God is doing in the larger circumstances and how God wants to accomplish his purpose through the man you are interceding for, you can test your prayers and be confident that you have heard God.

Think of God as the lifeguard at the pool mentioned above. While the mothers were gabbing, the lifeguard was watching the children, and saw the accident about to happen. The lifeguard was moving toward the scene, signaling for his colleague to help, even before the cry "Mommy" was uttered.

As the drama ensues, the lifeguard attends to the crisis yet continually scans the pools to make sure the dozens of other children remain safe.

God knows what needs to be done regarding the man for whom you are praying. God knew it before you and is acting in ways you cannot yet see. Your role in prayer is to find out how God wants you to direct your prayer energy.

When the mother reaches her child, she must get instructions from the lifeguard. So it is with us. We know a man in our life needs prayer, but God knows precisely what that prayer need is.

By now, you have regularly thanked God for the joy you have found in the man you are interceding for and have begun praying for God's will for him rather than your own intentions. I hope this process is changing your perspective. See yourself and the man you're praying for as part of God's plan that is much larger than either of you and unseen in full by either of you. Suspend your views about this man, your judgments, and pray for what God knows about him and desires for him even if that remains unknown to you. You want to work in harmony with God's power and move yourself—your desires for the man, your will, your evaluation of him—out of the way so you do not unwittingly block or impede God's work.

Our prayer work, so far, may feel as if you are praying in the dark. That is exactly as it needs to be. If you are still praying from your own knowledge, ideas, and assessments, you haven't grasped the power of effective intercessory prayer. Ask God to help you as you review the first six chapters.

Prayer 21
Lord Jesus, help me center myself on you. Take my focus off of my thoughts, my views, my way of looking at _____. I don't know how to separate myself from my own will, and I need your Holy Spirit to lead me in this process. I release my attachment to my own plans, desires, and outcomes for _____ and pray for your intentions for him that I can't yet know.

Learn
Yet, not what I will, but what you will.

Mark 14:36

Jesus prayed this prayer in the garden of Gethsemane before he was to die.

Unlearn
List the prayers you are currently praying that are *your* will for the man on whose behalf you are praying.

Prayer 22
Lord, show me your will and help me to replace each of these prayers [listed above] with ones that fit your larger purpose.

8

Praying for More of the Man He Is

Grow the godly qualities he already has

God's gifts and God's call are under full warranty—never canceled, never rescinded.

Romans 11:29 MSG

God's Spirit led an elder to pray for more of the quality this mother *thought* was her son's problem.

Mamie began praying for Leroi when he was in her womb. She didn't know he was a manchild and just prayed that the baby the Lord had given her would be born healthy and grow up to fear the Lord. For many years it looked as if the second part of her prayer would not be answered.

From his tumultuous teens onward, Leroi seemed to embrace everything radical and reject anything Christian. Awarded a full scholarship to their state's most prestigious university and then winning a coveted internship with a major corporation in New York, Leroi basked in the attention when Mamie told

him, "We're praying for you," but scoffed openly
at the possibility that there was potency to their
prayers. "There's no way my *grandmother's* religion can be right," he liked to laugh. He'd plant a
condescending kiss on Mamie's forehead before
leaving her and all "that old time religion" and
returning to the "real world."

Mamie, her sister Clara, and her mother put
"corns on their knees" praying for Leroi. As they
prayed harder and harder for him to "reject all that
head knowledge and come back to God," Leroi
became an agnostic, declaring it was impossible to
know God, then became a chanting Buddhist, and
finally adopted his own brand of religion that com-
bined his passion for LSD with his love for intellectual debate.

Mamie had raised her children in a sanctified
church and stressed unwavering faith in God.
"Why can't you just have faith?!" she shouted to
Leroi during one of his brief trips home, when he
refused to go to church with the family. He chose
instead to visit a psychic, whom he sought to
explain to him why his two close college friends
had recently come home in caskets, one from a
drug overdose, Mamie had heard, and the other
from something only hushed in secret but likely
related to his rumored homosexuality.

"Faith goes with feelings, Mama," he had crowed, strumming his guitar, in response to her demand. "I'm a man of my mind."

Mamie enlisted the prayer warriors at her small church to pray for Leroi. Elder Sass, who had been around the church since Mamie's mother was a girl, uttered a prayer for Leroi during a Wednesday night prayer meeting that made Mamie take notice.

"Lord God, sharpen Leroi's mind even more. Make him even more smart than he already is, smart enough to understand you, 'cause you're the only wise God, our Savior, Jesus Christ."

Leroi was too smart for his own good was what Mamie thought until she heard Elder Sass pray. She believed it was his intelligence that had turned him away from God. Sometimes she wished she had steered him away from the university and asked him to stay home, get a job to help out the family, and go to the junior college, where all that fancy philosophy and "God is dead stuff" wasn't taught. If she had asked him to give up college and work to help with the younger kids, he would have done it to make her happy. Now he sent money, but the help he provided was no comfort. She grieved the loss of her son's soul and feared the loss of his life, given what had become of his two friends.

And here was Elder Sass praying for his *mind*. On the way home from that prayer meeting, her mother and her sister Clara mentioned it.

"Did you ask Elder Sass to pray for Leroi?" Clara asked.

"Odd prayer she prayed, don't you think?" asked their mother, before Mamie could answer.

"Yes ma'am," was all Mamie could answer, as she pondered the words of the chief prayer warrior.

"Well, Elder Sass most times knows what to pray," her mother pronounced.

"Now that's for sure," seconded Clara.

"I reckon I'll pray for my grandson's mind then," her mother said, sensing her daughter's confusion and knowing her fear for her most successful son. "What you think, Mama Leroi?" her mother continued, addressing her daughter with the affectionate nickname she used with her children when she discussed her grandchildren.

Mamie couldn't answer. Her thought was on the caskets of Leroi's two too-smart friends.

"It can't hurt," said Clara. "Our prayers these last fifteen years haven't . . ."

"Just be still, Clara," their mother said. "From now on we're gonna pray for God to make Leroi smarter, smart enough to learn about the only wise God, our Savior, Jesus Christ."

They began to pray for Leroi in a new way. Leroi had the most brains of anybody in the family, even from the time he was in Head Start. They had never had to pray for his mind—his temper, appetites, attitudes, yes, but never his mind. Slowly Mamie began to realize she had never prayed for Christ to rule Leroi's mind, and she searched the Scriptures and discovered how much the Bible related the mind to faith. She prayed with new hope.

Mamie is convinced that it was because of those prayers for Leroi's mind that he became a Christian on Christmas sixteen years ago, a few years before her mother died, but about five years after Elder Sass died.

"I'm saved, Mama," he had said simply when he walked in the house, setting his luggage down and receiving his first hugs and kisses. He looked younger than he had during his last visit, and wiser. He went to church with them and during the sermon found the passages faster than anyone, using a leather Bible that had two entire columns of reference notes on every page and hundreds of pages at the back where you could look up words, subjects, and find who knows what else.

Leroi prayed the blessing for dinner his first evening home—a prayer by which they could *tell* he was indeed saved. He told them he had "received the Lord Jesus as his personal way to a relationship with the God of the Bible, the sovereign God of the universe."

"That mean you saved, right, boy?!" Mamie's mother asked.

"Yes ma'am!" he laughed, and shared that he made his confession of Christ at a Bible study group of actors, directors, and writers who met above a theater in New York City's Times Square.

Mamie couldn't imagine what *that* could have been like. Her mother just mumbled, "My Lord!" as the names of a few famous people rolled off Leroi's tongue.

But as he continued, the setting he described sounded more and more like church, only it was not *in* a church, and the elders were not called elders but did the same thing elders do—preach, teach, correct, and encourage. Leroi was reading the Bible from Genesis to Revelation in a year. Reading the Bible from cover to cover was something Mamie thought only the smartest preachers had done. But when she said so, Leroi replied patiently, "Anyone who can read can read the Bible, Mama."

"If my readin' was good, I'd sure try it," chimed Mamie's mother.

"Gramma, I'll send you a mini-boombox and the entire Bible on cassettes. You can listen to the Bible as I read it."

Mamie's eyes got teary as her mother and son hugged, and they burst into laughing sobs when Leroi said, "Hey, why is everybody so surprised? This *is,* after all, my *grandmother's* religion."

———■———

Once we have fully suspended our own ideas of what God needs to do in the men we are praying for, we can pray for the man he *is*. We can see the godly qualities he already exhibits. Our interceding prayers will give us more and more of God's perspective. As we catch glimpses of godly qualities in him from God's point of view, we can begin to pray for *more* of those. So many Christian women are looking for changes to result from our prayers, but we must pray as we notice *godly qualities,* not as we notice *changes.*

Let's base our prayers on God's creation of our men. God's creation is good but flawed by human disobedience (Genesis 1–3). The men we are praying for are good because they were created by God. Yes, they are flawed, but so is our view of them because we are also flawed. Jesus addressed this quite graphically in Matthew 7:3–5:

> Why do you look at the speck of sawdust in your brother's eye and pay no attention to the plank in your own eye? How can you say to your brother, "Let me take the speck out of your eye,"

when all the time there is a plank in your own
eye? You hypocrite, first take the plank out of
your own eye, and then you will see clearly to
remove the speck from your brother's eye.

These words hit us pretty hard, but they apply
to all of us when we seek God's view of the husbands, fathers, sons, friends, pastors, and other
men in our lives—as opposed to television, movies,
romance novels, and other views we have formed
of who we think these men should be.

There is something of God in every human being
because we are created in his image. Carefully consider the man you are praying for—even if he does
not have a relationship with God—and list his
godly qualities. Remember, the "gifts . . . of God are
without repentance," (Romans 11:29 KJV); we all
have gifts whether or not we are in right standing
with God.

Your list probably contains the things you like
about him, similar to the one you made in chapter 6.
Make the list from God's perspective. That means
you understand that a godly quality may exhibit
itself in sinful or problematic behavior, since sin, simply put, is an inappropriate response to a legitimate
need or a wrongful expression of a God-given urge.

Here's an example: My friend's husband is very
streetwise. That quality served them well as they
bought a building in a "turning" neighborhood that

had been seized by drug-dealers. He was able to handle a situation that made other potential homeowners afraid to purchase real estate in that community. In a short time, the neighborhood was designated a historic landmark district and their investment in their building multiplied phenomenally.

At the same time, my friend agonized over the streetwise quality in her husband as he took on business challenges with the same intuitive risk-taking. Often he was successful, but other times his endeavors produced only losses.

Courage and strong intuition were among his qualities, but my friend needed to ask God to show her more of her husband's godly courage and pray for God's Spirit to guide her husband's intuition.

Rather than praying for new qualities that we want to see in men, ones that are likely based on culture, selfishness, or ungodly media, we want to pray for God to take hold of the qualities these men already have. This means not only overlooking our own perspectives, but looking beyond outward appearances and circumstances deep into the core qualities of the man.

If the man you are praying for works long hours at a demanding job or jobs that cut into time you'd prefer he spent with you and the family, you might have labored in prayer that the Lord "help him stop being a workaholic" or specifically that he "come home for dinner with the family" as you watch him become more and more like a visitor to your home and children. You've learned in chapter 6 to appreciate that he is a good provider and thank God continually for the material and financial joys you and your kids experience as a result.

Now, after seeking God's perspective, you understand that being a good provider is one of this man's godly qualities. One of God's names in Hebrew is translated Jehovah Jireh, which means the Lord is our provider. Instead of praying for change, pray that he be strengthened as a godly provider.

As you pray that God will strengthen and enhance the man's God-given qualities, God may reveal to you ways to pray. For example, you might pray that he help provide for others, or that he be used by God in his work, or that this quality bring God glory.

If you are praying for a behavior change—"that he stop working overtime and spend more time with the family"—rather than for God to manage his God-given gifts and abilities, you are not praying for the man he is, but rather some image of the man you want him to be. He's already created in God's image. You have no power, even with your most sincere prayers, to remake him according to the image you want, and you have no right to ask God to do so.

You do have the wonderful privilege of prayer to put your energy in harmony with God's power. You do that by recognizing his inner qualities and praying that they be enhanced and displayed as God intends.

Prayer 23
Lord, give me insight into the godly qualities you created in _____. Help me discern his godly qualities that right now may be exercised in sinful behavior. Turn the gifts you created in him toward you and develop his gifts fully according to your purpose.

Learn
We live by faith, not by sight.

2 Corinthians 5:7

Unlearn
The following is a list of common prayer wishes women bring to God about their husbands, sons, brothers, and fathers. Next to each concern is another way to look at that characteristic. Use it to discover existing qualities in the man you are interceding for and pray for him to be more of the man God created him to be.

I See	God Sees
sleeps too much	is at peace with himself
works all the time	is a good provider
hangs out with the boys	is a loyal friend

is not affectionate enough	is self-contained
spends too much money	is generous
gives too much time to others	is compassionate
is a know-it-all	values understanding
needs salvation	has needs only God can fill
_____	_____
_____	_____
_____	_____

Substitute what you see with what God sees in the prayer below.

Prayer 24

Lord, you have gifted _____ with the quality of being at peace with himself. Thank you for all of his wonderful qualities—those I recognize and those that I don't yet perceive. Multiply his quality of being at peace with himself and therefore able to sleep, and bring it into godly balance so he brings you glory.

9

Recognizing Answered Prayers

Look for and see answered prayers

Prayer frees us to be controlled by God.
Richard Foster, *Freedom of Simplicity*

God replaced a daughter's desire for *answers* to her prayers for her dad with *intimacy* with God and her father.

Tiffany gave her dad's hand a tight squeeze and placed a gentle kiss on his bald head as she wheeled him onto the wheelchairs-only balcony overlooking the golf course. He could walk, but the wheelchair was his way of protesting that the best view was reserved exclusively for "wheelies."

"D— if I'll be penalized 'cause I've kept my Army build!" he said.

She thanked God that she could afford such great care for him and that her job allowed her the freedom to leave early on Tuesday and Friday afternoons, his favorite visiting days. "Not so d— many once-in-whilers," he said, referring to the occasional visitors most of the residents received. She understood it was his way of thanking her for her regular visits. He'd never say thank you directly.

The orderly served their lunch as they enjoyed the soft afternoon sun and the peaceful view of the greens. "God is gracious, God is good, and we thank him for our food. Amen," her father prayed.

Eighty-five years old, thought Tiffany, *still wholly in charge of his faculties and still praying the same grace he learned when he was five.* She giggled and squeezed his hand. No one ever expected or, frankly, wanted him to outlive her mother, and only she among her siblings, who were among the d— once-in-whilers, had forgiven him for it.

"Why are the sweet so weak and wicked so strong?" her oldest brother had remarked when he was told that their mother had died and their hard-drinking, gambling, irascible father had declared himself unable to live in the house without her.

She had discovered her own love for her father a full decade after she learned about God's love for her. At a women's retreat, the salvation message she had come to take for granted had become starkly real to her. "It is only because of Jesus that I'm able to even relate to God," she had mused on the bus ride home from the lofty spiritual getaway. "Holiness is perfection. There's no way God could have anything to do with me if it weren't for Jesus." The unsavory thought that she and her father shared the same condition—sin—flickered, out of nowhere, in her brain. The idea brought her breakfast to her throat, and she had to swallow real hard to get rid of the unpleasant taste. That was the first change in her thinking.

After her mother died, she had routinely prayed that her fragmented siblings would become a real family and be able to forgive their dad. With the loss of her "sainted" mother, she had learned to accept God's sovereignty. It was a hard lesson.

After the retreat, bit by bit, imperceptibly, she began to view herself, her siblings, and her "devilish dad" all in the same camp, a camp of sinners, none holy. Her prayer simplified to, "Help us be a family, Lord."

As she tightened her grip on the discipline of prayer, and most important, opened her prayer times to *listening* to God, her utterances became, "Show me, Lord Jesus, how to be a godly part of this family." One day a prayer she had never anticipated leapt from her lips, "Lord, show me how to be a good daughter." She wept as she heard her own words.

Her tears were angry, not only with her father but with God. How could God be so unfair? Why should *she* have to measure up in any way compared to that philanderer! But the tears also came from a sadness deep inside that she could not, at the time, plumb.

"Nothin' but wimmin', wimmin', wimmin' here." She half-listened to his complaints there on the balcony. "They all want a man and gat nothin' ta catch a man wit. Tif, it's tough here being almost the onliest able-bodied male. And they talk, talk, talk ..." While she listened with a contented smile, she reflected that she *was* glad Dad was still around. Soon he'd slide into reminiscences about her mom, and she'd tune her eager ears to hear the same old stories for the nth time, more embellished than ever. She savored every moment with the old guy whom she, and all her siblings, had despised growing up with.

Tiffany now understood that it was God's Spirit at work in that tearful prayer. After that, her fond memories of her grandparents contained a character who had heretofore been absent—her father as a little boy, a teen, and a young man. The stories they told weren't idyllic anymore, not when viewed through what must have been her father's experience. He had always hated to talk about his youth. "I live in the present," he'd say, clamping his teeth on a cigar. She began to see that the "good old days" and "our old ways" to her grandparents were poverty, danger, nonchalant immorality, and ugly challenge to a youth who had only his own verve to define his manhood.

As Tiffany let the Lord change her, she was stunned to find her view of her father so drastically changed. Her childhood had left her hurt and needing healing that only Jesus had been able to accomplish. "Dad, you're just like me," she blurted out one day to the streaming water in her shower. She had just finished her morning prayer time. The revelation was like an emotional fountain. "Only you've had to be tough so long you can't cry at the cross like me." Then she had whispered, "But Lord, you already understood that."

"Listen here, Tif," her dad said as she wheeled him back inside after lunch. "There's a whole box of letters and stuff you might want to take. H—, I don't have time to look at all that stuff. Your ma, bless her sweet soul, kept all that crap you kids sent home from college and where-in-the-h—-ever you all were. I ain't wrote that many letters from that pit Korea as you kids wrote from them luxury scholarship dormitories. But your ma kept all 'at stuff. It's in a big box down by reception. Take it or it's going out in the trash."

"Okay, Dad."

He stood at the elevator and held her in a bear hug so long that no one in sight could miss it and then said loud enough for the deaf to hear that *he* had regular visitors, "That's my girl, Tif. See ya Friday. Don't forget my Lucky Strikes." He paused, then continued in a tone so pitiful one would think he was in Alcatraz, not an expensive retirement home, "They got nuthin' in here. Nuthin', Tif."

Tiffany always stopped in the lovely chapel on the first floor to pray, and today as she knelt before the plain, unadorned altar, she thanked God for her family and especially her father. "Thank you for bringing him through everything he's been through, giving him long life, Lord. Keep him healthy and strong. Please heal the rift between Dad and the other kids. Thank you for helping me see him as you see him, Lord, and for giving me a new heart toward him." She knelt in peaceful silence a long time.

An orderly carried the box to her car. With the trunk door open she sorted through the trove of letters, all addressed to her father, from his children—all three sets, those by her mom, his wife, and his "outside kids" as he referred to those from his liaisons. Not a single one was opened. "What a character," she said aloud, unfazed.

One letter she had written years ago caught her eye, and sitting in the driver seat she ripped it open.

Dad,

I've tried to will this away, but for years it's been bothering me. I've worked and prayed to forgive, not to let it be a bitter root in me, but I don't feel I've been very successful at forgiving, and the bitterness seems to come out in horribly unloving speech and actions toward you, often when I least expect it.

So, I'm just going to bring it to you. Maybe you can shed some light on it that my fourteen-year-old self was not able to see. Perhaps I have misunderstood something crucial, and once I understand I will be able to let go of the hurt and unravel the pain I have let sprinkle into almost everything, at least related to you and men, over the years.

Dad, do you remember one morning when I was still in grade school when the phone rang and I answered it? You answered it too, from the cellar, but you didn't realize I had already picked up the receiver upstairs. I don't remember much of the call because it numbed me. It was another woman, and you talked to her in a way I knew, even at that age, husbands should only speak to wives. I ran downstairs and confronted you, saying I was going to tell Mom. I will never forget what you said, "Why do you want to tell her? It's only going to hurt her. Let's just keep this between us."

Dad, I cannot state all the repercussions of those words because they have affected so much of my life. I view that moment as my personal loss of innocence.

I want to write what this incident meant, but I don't honestly know what it meant to me. It still hurts to the point of tears to remember it even now. The world became a different place. I lived and still live a lie every day with Mom. Each time a man disappoints me, I have a huge storage bin, created that day, in which to store the disappointment.

My ability to be your little girl—a "daddy's girl," as folks used to call me—ended with this incident. I could no longer race to the front door and greet you with a big hug when you came home. I could no longer listen to your opinions as the sage in my life. I wish the childhood father you were to me could always have been mine. I wish our relationship had metamorphosed into something even sweeter with time, as I became a teenager and a woman. I still want my daddy, the man I knew as my father before that phone call. Perhaps open honesty is the next best thing to innocence.

> Please let's talk, Dad.
> Love,
> Tif

She tossed the letter she had long ago forgotten about into the trash can as she exited the parking lot. "Thank you, Lord, for healing," prayed Tiffany, as she started the engine.

Prayer released the power in Tiffany to enable her to love her dad; prayer opened the way to healing her relationship with him; prayer allowed her to get over the wounds he dealt her in the past; prayer helped her build strong fellowship with him; prayer worked! Tiffany and her dad illustrate the five valuable results of prayer.

Prayer . . .

- releases the power in us,
- unleashes God's power and purpose in our relationships,
- heals wounds,
- builds strong community and encourages others, and
- works!

As we pray, we discover that our role in looking for and seeing answered prayers is almost a dichotomy. We start praying because we want answers. But as we pray, we discover that we want God. Theologian Richard Foster puts it beautifully when he said that we "change the image flow from God coming into us to our coming into God." We begin praying for the men in our lives because we want God to come into our situation. As we continue to pray, we end up coming into God's plan.

Praying for the men in our lives often starts with a list of talking points with which we approach our Lord, almost a to-do list for God. But if we open ourselves to counsel like that in this little book, these "gimme chats" morph into fellowship. Where once we had to push ourselves to pray, it becomes hard not to pray; we utter snatch prayers constantly and feel out-of-sorts when we miss our devotion dates.

We begin to delight in knowing God through prayer itself. The answers to prayer become secondary, even forgotten.

Often women who begin to labor in prayer, who make prayer a serious part of their lives, say they later stumble on the positive answers to prayers they had made much earlier and then had forgotten. They had become detached from the outcome and attached to the process of communicating with God. Instead of looking for a "yes" or "no" or even "wait" answer to their prayers, these women began enjoying a sweet fellowship with God through prayer. And that fellowship transforms what to others would be waiting or suffering or disappointment into a joy (Nehemiah 8:10) that has nothing to do with their circumstances or the men in their lives. The very act of praying transforms the need for answers to prayer into a peace (Philippians 4:7) that has nothing logically to do with the situations they were praying about—with fathers, brothers, husbands, sons, and male friends.

Women who pray also begin to accept the role we play in the lives of the men for whom we are praying. Through our intimacy with God, we join in what God is doing, as Henry T. Blackaby and Claude V. King express so beautifully in *Experiencing God*. We become a team player on the team that is destined to win, rather than trying to be quarterback of our own team of often unwilling players.

> I gave up all that inferior stuff so I could *know Christ personally*, experience his resurrection power, be a partner in his suffering, and go all the way with him to death itself.

Philippians 3:10 MSG (emphasis added)

God answers prayer. We must tune ourselves to receive the answers, knowing we started praying because God initiated it. Our prayers were in response to God. Once we understand that we were not praying because of the men in our lives, we were praying in response to God's call, we can see through our prayers, what God is doing in our men, and in us in preparation for the coming of Jesus Christ.

Prayer 25
Lord, I want to know, feel, and live what others are talking about when they describe how wonderful it is to just experience you in prayer. You know my requests for _____, but for this moment, this prayer, I'm open to whatever you want to do in the inner me so I can be your friend.

Learn
I no longer call you servants. . . . Instead, I have called you friends.

John 15:15

Unlearn
Instead of looking for answers to your prayers, look for a closer connection to God.

Prayer 26
Thank you for all the answered prayers, Lord. You are too amazing for words. Thank you for the yes answers that are over and above all that I could ask or imagine. Thank you for the no answers that I now understand were the right answers. I'm grateful for your wisdom. And I appreciate with anticipation the answers I cannot yet hear or see. I know you have answered every prayer already!

Reflect back on your prayers and your experience with this book. How has your view of the man you are praying for changed since you read this book? How has your attitude changed? Have you seen changes in yourself? In the man for whom you are praying? How is God answering your prayers for your man? How is God changing you in the process?

Prayer 27
Thank you, Lord, for the wonderful adventure that praying through life is!

Prayers
A Devotional Guide

———■———

For your reflection time, the prayers in this book are repeated below. These prayers are not a formula for godliness. You don't need to pray them word-for-word or even pray every one. Rather, they are suggestions to help you learn to work in concert with the Holy Spirit to change your heart and life, and perhaps affect the man you are praying for.

Father Prayer 1

Great God, Creator of the universe, you who made me, hear this prayer and let me—through Jesus Christ—connect with you intimately as your daughter. I yield whatever is in me that hinders our relationship, including anything involving my natural father. I leave all such hindrances at the foot of the cross, because they are sins Jesus has already handled. I trust your Spirit's work, with time, to heal me of all the results of these sins and to enlarge my capacity to be your beloved daughter and experience you as my Daddy-God.

Father Prayer 2

Lord, thank you for a deeper understanding of just how important Dad has been in my life. He has given me a glimpse of you, making it easier for me to relate to you. Bless him richly! Let Dad's and my relationship be a basis for my understanding of the men on whose behalf I will offer prayer.

Brother Prayer

Lord, you created kinship order—and have placed me in this family—for a purpose. I open myself to your intent in giving me these blood ties. As you grow me as a Christian "sister," help me to be an exemplary natural sister and remove any barriers between me and my brothers that hinder prayer and block blessings.

Husband Prayer

Lord, may my husband trust me without reserve and never have reason to regret it. May he be greatly respected.

Son Prayer

Lord God, my son was your son first. You knit him together in my womb. As much as I love him, your love for him is even greater. So, I place him before you in spirit as wholly yours. Let my attitude toward my son be as Mary's when you made her the mother of Jesus, "I'm the Lord's maid, ready to serve" (Luke 1:38 MSG).

Spiritual Brother Prayer

I pray that out of your glorious riches you will strengthen my brothers in Christ with power through your Spirit in their inner beings. Christ, dwell in their hearts through faith. And I pray that my brothers, being rooted and established in love, may have power united with all of us Christians.

Allow them to grasp how wide and long and high and deep is your love, Christ Jesus. Let them experience this love that surpasses knowledge and be filled with you, dear God.

Prayer 1

Lord, show me the men you want me to pray for. Enable me to pray for them. Equip me to pray for them effectively.

Prayer 2

1 Thessalonians 5: 15–19 Acrostic Prayer

Pardon me and _____ for our sins and shortcomings.

Restore us to **R**ight relationship with you and with each other.

Th**A**nks for _____ _____.

My jo**Y** overflows because of ____ _____.

Lord, I op**E**n myself to the work of your Spirit.

With deep **R**espect for prophecy, I know you will reveal to me what I need to know to pray in your will and work in harmony with my prayers.

Prayer 3

Lord, I know you will bring about the change I have prayed for because I am willing to be changed in whatever way you wish.

Prayer 4

Lord, you have not given me feelings of fear or of [add your own feelings], but you have given me a sense of power, love, and mental stability.

Prayer 5

Lord, show me how I need to change in each of the instances I have listed above. I am willing to be changed in whatever way you wish, and I need you to reveal to me, as I study and meditate on the Bible, pray, and talk with other Christians, what those changes you desire in me are and how I can change.

Prayer 6

Lord, show me how to pray for _____. Help me not to judge his needs, but teach me how to listen to his concerns and to discern what you want me to pray for on his behalf. Show me how to pray in harmony with your will and pray with respect for the issues about which he has expressed concern.

Prayer 7

Lord, give me ears to hear _____'s words, as well as his thoughts and feelings underneath the words.

Move me out of the way of _____'s expressing himself. Replace my reactions with the empathy of Jesus to what he says and how he says it.

Lord, please identify in me the habits that prevent _____ from opening up to me and let your Spirit in me replace them with new ways that will make me an irresistible listener.

Prayer 8

Lord, you are the great hearer of prayer and discerner of thoughts. Give me abounding love for _____ as a fruit of your Spirit. With that spirit of love, give me the gift of discernment so I will be able to pray what is pleasing to you, to pray for your perfect will on his behalf, and to operate in harmony with my prayers.

Prayer 9

Lord, show me what to say or not say in each of the instances I have listed above, so I can genuinely hear the true needs for prayer. Reveal to me, through your gift of discernment, what you desire as my prayers for each of these men.

Prayer 10

Lord, prepare me to be an intercessor for _____. Thank you for giving me the privilege of being one small connector between your plans for him and the outworking of those plans.

Prayer 11

Lord Jesus, I submit myself to you, empty of motives and plans for _____. Show me what you want me to pray on his behalf. And until I am confident I have heard from you, Lord, I pray simply that your plans for him become his reality.

Prayer 12

Lord Jesus, you said that whatever we bind on

earth will be bound in heaven, and whatever we loose on earth will be loosed in heaven. With this prayer, I bind _____ in _____'s life. And, Lord, I loose _____ to be free to relate to you directly in prayer on his own behalf.

Prayer 13

Lord Jesus, help me to decrease as you increase.

Prayer 14

Lord, teach me to pray.

Prayer 15

You've told me to be joyful about _____, and I know there are things about him that bring joy to your heart, Lord. Show me those facets of him via your Holy Spirit, and let me have the joy of appreciating those qualities in him.

Prayer 16

Thank you, Lord Jesus, for [one of your joys in the man for whom you are praying]. Thank you for revealing this part of his nature to me. You created him, and I'm glad to know him and to share in his good qualities.

Prayer 17

[Be in silence with God for whatever time your schedule permits.]

Prayer 18

Sovereign Lord, you know _____
far better than I do. Thank you for his _____
and other things you have shown me about him
that bring me joy. You created him. You sustain
his life. You have a wonderful purpose for him.
Show me what you specifically want me to pray
for regarding _____ . Allow me to
help accomplish *your* will in him through this
prayer.

Prayer 19

Lord, I admit that I am not living in a way that
pleases you regarding [name your problem area].
I realize this sin problem is making it impossible
for us to communicate clearly. I know you hear
my prayer, but I can't hear you, God. Please help
me offer my body as a living sacrifice, holy and
pleasing to you as my act of worship that will
open up our lines of communication.

Prayer 20

Lord, thank you for _____'s fine
qualities such as _____ that make
me know I need to keep speaking to him with
real respect [or add other quality of godly speech]
and acting _____ [add other quality
of godly behavior] toward him. I am humbled by
how you are changing my attitude and behavior,
and I know this is opening me up to hear with
clarity your intentions for him so I can pray in
harmony with your will.

Prayer 21

Lord Jesus, help me center myself on you. Take my focus off of my thoughts, my views, my way of looking at _____. I don't know how to separate myself from my own will, and I need your Holy Spirit to lead me in this process. I release my attachment to my own plans, desires, and outcomes for _____ and pray for your intentions for him that I can't yet know.

Prayer 22

Lord, show me your will and help me to replace each of these prayers [listed above] with ones that fit your larger purpose.

Prayer 23

Lord, give me insight into the godly qualities you created in _____. Help me discern his godly qualities that right now may be exercised in sinful behavior. Turn the gifts you created in him toward you and develop his gifts fully according to your purpose.

Prayer 24

Lord, you have gifted _____ with the quality of being at peace with himself. Thank you for all of his wonderful qualities—those I recognize and those that I don't yet perceive. Multiply his quality of being at peace with himself and therefore able to sleep, and bring it into godly balance so he brings you glory.

Prayer 25

Lord, I want to know, feel, and live what others are talking about when they describe how wonderful it is to just experience you in prayer. You know my requests for _____, but for this moment, this prayer, I'm open to whatever you want to do in the inner me so I can be your friend.

Prayer 26

Thank you for all the answered prayers, Lord. You are too amazing for words. Thank you for the yes answers that are over and above all that I could ask or imagine. Thank you for the no answers that I now understand were the right answers. I'm grateful for your wisdom. And I appreciate with anticipation the answers I cannot yet hear or see. I know you have answered every prayer already!

Prayer 27

Thank you, Lord, for the wonderful adventure that praying through life is!

Recommended Reading

Henry T. Blackaby and Claude V. King, *Experiencing God* (Nashville: LifeWay Press, 1990).

Richard Foster, *Celebration of Discipline* (San Francisco: HarperSanFrancisco, 1978).

Richard Foster, *Freedom of Simplicity* (New York: HarperCollins, 1981).

C. S. Lewis, *Mere Christianity* (New York: Touchstone, 1943).

Michael P. Nichols, *The Lost Art of Listening* (New York: Guilford Press, 1995).

Rosalind Rinker, *Prayer* (Grand Rapids: Zondervan, 1959).

Bruce Waltke, *Knowing the Will of God* (Eugene, Ore.: Harvest House, 1998).

Scripture Index

Acknowledgments

———

Throughout my entire life I've been blessed with praying men. I have also encountered some powerful praying women. I wish to acknowledge the following for their prayers and wonderful help in the publication of this book: Sandra VanderZicht and the wonderful team at Zondervan, and Adrienne Ingrum, who lovingly and supportively gets the job done and continues to open doors for authors.

No words can aptly acknowledge the men in my life, for whom I pray and who pray for me: my husband, Ronald Cook; our sons, Samuel David and Christopher Daniel; and all the men of the Bronx Christian Fellowship Church family.

I praise God for the opportunity to let these words of prayer live. May it transform your prayer life.

Become "Ms. Right" Before You Find "Mr. Right."

A New Dating Attitude
Getting Ready for the Mate God Has for You

Dr. Suzan D. Johnson Cook

Use the Beatitudes to change your own attitudes as you wait for the mate God is preparing for you.

The number of people who wish they were married is myriad. Dating clubs, newspaper columns, and books on how to find a mate are everywhere. But no one has addressed this deep desire like Dr. Suzan D. Johnson Cook. She approaches this aching need and difficult situation from both a spiritual and practical perspective, applying the Beatitudes to the number one preoccupation of most single, divorced, and widowed Christian women—how to find a husband.

This book uses the Beatitudes as a platform for those who are ready for the good news of God's way to kiss the single life good-bye. Pastor Johnson Cook encourages readers to develop what she calls "betrothal attitudes"—positive states of mind and qualities of character that will help the reader enjoy her single life while she is becoming the person she needs to be to receive the mate God has in store for her.

These "betrothal attitudes" are spiritual teachings and life lessons learned by the author and others in her life, lessons that show how healing and victory can come to those who are willing to wait on God, receive God's teaching, and develop new attitudes toward themselves and their relationships.

Softcover: 0-310-23532-4